CALL
of the
CRICKET

CALL
of the
CRICKET

Irwin "Larry" Altman

CELESTIAL ARTS
Millbrae, California

Library of Congress Cataloging in Publication Data

Altman, Larry, 1928-
     The call of the cricket.

     1. Altman, Larry, 1928-   2. Swindlers and swindling—Biography.   I. Title.
HV6248.A38A33   364.1'63'0924 [B]   77-90018
ISBN 0-89087-216-3

1   2   3   4   5   6—82   81   80   79   78

Dedication:

To my wife

Acknowledgments

Dean Gregory gave me books and encouragement. Steve Northrup and Jack Burris showed faith in me. David Morris directed me ruthlessly and squeezed sense out of the manuscript. The entire staff at Celestial Arts made me feel as though I belonged—even when I delivered the manuscript in a tattered shopping bag. Jane Falk, Marc Elliot, Lou, and Sam know why their names are here. My good friend A. D. Winans, poet, editor, publisher of *Second Coming*, a literary magazine, is to be thanked for permission to quote from his poem "America." Mostly I thank A. D. for his friendship and all the letters he wrote me while I was in Folsom Prison.

Names and places have been changed and some events are dramatizations. But the people in the book are very real and I thank them for having added to my life.

Finally, I shall always be indebted to T.

Irwin "Larry" Altman
San Francisco

Prologue

On the day I left Folsom Prison, I wasn't thinking about writing a book about my life as a gentleman-thief, swindler, and bigamist. A million crazy thoughts screwed with my head that day, but nothing so grandiose as spewing my life's debris over neat pages for the world to sift through. Sure, I had an attack of the crazies that day: shakes, fears, vivid paranoid pictures of people staring and knowing I just got out of the *joint* . . . breaking out in nervous sweats because my new street clothes were baggy . . . worrying about if my prick would stand up that night, and what to say to my wife if it didn't. I can talk about it *all* now. But that day, over a year ago, I didn't have writing in mind.

See: Leaving prison is always a suspenseful bureaucratic "maybe." All I wanted was to get the fuck out of there before some bull or office clerk—or anyone else with authority over a convict—decided I should stay another day or so, "Just to be sure everything's in order."

"In order" meant that since I was serving a federal and state sentence at one crack in Folsom, they wanted to be damned certain that the federal government would go along with my state parole and not require me to serve the remaining federal sentence which would have been eight months. The teletype from the federal government didn't come in until the exact day I was to be released on state parole. Until that time no one knew if the U.S. marshal would come after me, or if I'd be allowed to get going with my parole. The teletype said: "No longer wanted" and I said, "Good, God damnit, my time's up, let me out."

And, let me out they did. At the main gate, when the trust officer—the man who watches over any money a poor son-of-a-bitchin' convict may have accumulated—handed me two-hundred dollars saying, "Here's your mustering-out pay." I wanted to say "Fuck you very much," but I didn't. A remark like that could cost another five days behind the walls. I did say, "Hope I don't get robbed on the way home." Which struck me funny. But not him. He could only say, sternly, "Better be careful with this money. The state doesn't have money to be pissing away on cons who can't take care of themselves."

The taxpayers cough up sixteen million dollars a year to maintain Folsom Prison—a "warehouse" for "hopeless" criminals. A major portion of the money is payroll for a staff of about five hundred employees, many of whom are related to each other. Five hundred people, most of them bland and humorless. But, the two-hundred dollars mustering-out money doesn't come out of the tax chest. It comes out of the twenty-five percent deducted from the sales of prisoners' creative works, such as paintings and leathercraft and so forth. And it comes out of the profits from the "goodies" sold in the prison canteen: tobacco, candy, canned meats, powdered dairy products, jellies, and hot peppers, and instant coffee.

I had been home two months when a clerk discovered a snag. A goof. A fuck-up. Seems as though they let me go eight months too soon . . . "really embarrassing . . . we *know* how you must feel but you must go back . . . ." In a pig's ass—they knew! I made the painful decision to become a fugitive once more. I wasn't going back to the insanity of prison. Not without having committed a crime.

The years of waiting and believing didn't pay off after all. Not because I didn't want it to. But because bureaucracy demanded the surrender of my happiness. They wanted me to pay for their mistake. As far as I was concerned, they could hang their dirty underwear elsewhere. I wasn't going back.

Surviving as a fugitive, without stealing to eat, is almost impossible when you start out broke. I had 50 dollars. One change of clothes. No wheels. I couldn't go near people I knew, or places I'd been known to frequent. My I.D. was useless. In a matter of moments, my face, complete physical description—including my habits and hobbies and what kind of smokes I use—would be wired to police agencies, airline terminals, bus stations, large motel chains, and post offices all around the country. Even with the deck stacked against me in every direction and knowing how already miserable problems would grow to almost unsurmountable proportions, I decided it was better than decaying in a cramped prison cage.

My life once again depended on how quickly and cleverly I could manage pending disasters: What would I do if I had no roof, food, or bed? Walking the streets at night, aimlessly, is a sure way to get busted. Even the Salvation Army requires at least a Social Security card for a bunk and food. Getting work, even as a dishwasher or mop-up man is hard as hell when you're dirty, unshaven and don't have identification of some kind. Begging for change is honorable. But it stinks when you're running scared and paranoid.

In my stealing days I could handle any personal disaster. Simple. I'd steal. But this time there was something different. I lost my desire to steal. Listen. Let me tell you. I spent over twenty years with my hands in and out of pockets and panties from coast to coast. And I can do it again—better than before. And I know how to seemingly disappear off the face of the planet. Sure, I'll tell you how. If you're finding life dull, I can sure as shit show you how to stir it up. I'll show you. Step by step. But don't ask me to go with you. As I said, I've lost my desire for that kind of excitement. It's been replaced with a new and burning desire motivated by a strange feeling I buried 35 years ago when my father died. A feeling I could not seem to dig up again until that day when bureaucratic error opened the grave and let it out. It's pure anger. How exciting it is to know what it's like to be really pissed off!

So, I was a fugitive, and I wasn't going to steal to survive. Somehow, I wound up in Modesto, California, with three dollars left out of the fifty. Other than the three dollars, my only other possession was a disposable razor I kept in my back pocket. My only change of clothes and a toothbrush were left behind in a motel. Modesto weather is always hot. I smelled like a person who hadn't bathed for a couple of days. And, I needed a shave.

Two things happened that day. I shaved in a gas station restroom. I got a job washing dishes in the Dinner-Bell Cafe on South 7th for $2.25 an hour. The boss, a guy named Carl, asked me one question, "Can you work that goddamn washin' machine?" I could. I worked that day. Got paid that night. Got a cheap room in a motel near the cafe that caters to farm laborers. Lousy mattress, beer cans thrown around, and the toilet was a slow flusher. But, I didn't care. My intuition said I'd make it.

Learning that I didn't have to steal to live only reinforced my anger. I wanted to be totally free. Home with my family. And that's all I thought about for the next year. Many times I thought of surrendering. And I even went to an attorney for advice. I had to take a chance, tell someone. So, I played Russian roulette with the telephone book, picked an attorney out of the Yellow Pages, and went to see him. Not only did he advise me that I would be a fool to surrender, but he let me know that the whole damned thing was legally absurd.

"If you're stupid enough to surrender," he said, "you give up any right to a hearing. They'll dump you right into the joint . . . think they want the papers to tell people they goofed?"

How would it feel? I can tell you. I lived it. And surprisingly I found many people who were willing to help me see it through and not turn me over to the law. Not thieves, either. But men and women who always worked hard for their keep. Responsible community-minded people. I found out. These kinds of people do exist. There was only one man, "Doc" Prudent, who tried to take advantage of my vulnerable position as an ex-con fugitive. Until he came into my life I thought I held a fairly high position in the world of con games. Happily, I admit that if there is such a title as "Grand Old Man of Con," he deserves it.

I took the attorney's advice. Sat still. Got a better paying job. Went into business with Doc . . . and began to believe that Horatio Alger way is possible, even these days. I tried to make it as easy as possible for the law to find me. And, after almost a year, when I began to wonder if they had given up, the relief came: I was arrested.

Standing in front of the judge, listening to prosecuting and defense attorneys present arguments, knowing that there were not less than 20 people in that court room who had come to speak in my behalf, and knowing that I had given the system the proper amount of jail time, and knowing with certainty that if things went wrong, a crusade in my behalf would erupt picket-line style, I was confident.

After deciding the whole mess was not only absurd but also confusing, the judge decided that the prison system should get their papers in the proper order, let him know when and if they did; but in the meanwhile he could see no just cause for me to be detained in jail.

As Clifford Tedman, my court-appointed attorney says, "It may take a hundred years for them to straighten out the mess . . . you know . . . coffee breaks . . . vacation . . . but in the meantime you're free."

My life has always been like a jigsaw puzzle that I could never quite put together. Furthermore, until now I never really tried. Not really. Now that I'm attempting to make the pieces lock, open old doors, see the people I've hurt on my way to prison, remembering family, friends, tears and a few laughs, I find myself feeling more than the anger that opened up last year. I feel caring, tenderness, concern, outrage at injustice, and I feel purpose. Best of all, I am becoming a feeling person. Again.

No, when I left Folsom Prison, and even for a time afterward, I didn't give any thought to writing a book. But I can tell you about my life as I lived it. I can tell you about that day in San Diego, when a stranger and I decided in a seemingly casual way to bilk a bank. His bank. That was a long time ago. A lot of years have passed since then.

Then, especially, I had no intention of writing a book.

Writing about it: keeping a daily diary or notes stuck away in pants pockets and dresser drawers would have been the height of insanity or at least stupidity. Writing about it would have been a goddamn good way to leave a cross- country trail of clues for the cops if I had lost even one note.

Hell, I was too busy stealing, screwing, and running to write. And when I wasn't doing those things I was too tired to write. So, now I'm digging all the notes out of my head. The banks—big and little. The women—fancy and not so fancy. The drugstore chain executive who tried to sell me his wife because he was deep in debt. At that time I was posing as a department store heir for the purpose of getting my hands on some of the drugstore's money.

Posing or being an impostor came to me easily. Part of my early childhood training included a course in drama. My Rumanian-gypsy grandfather wanted me to have "culture." He never had any idea, I'm certain, as to how I would eventually use the broad spectrum of philosophies, religions, and cultures—East and West, he shared with me. He was my mother's father. As a young man he gave up gypsy life, settled down, and amassed a tidy fortune. He shared with me also his thinking in regard to the ladies which served to get me into many a bedroom and many a marriage. My marriages all ended without benefit of divorce. My present marriage of twenty-three years is my only legal one.

I can tell you about a childhood of conflicts. I was a fat kid raised in a world of mostly skinny people. I can tell you how I felt when I discovered that my father—a huge, well-proportioned man—couldn't stand the sight of his fat son. And I can tell you what it's like to learn to lie to keep him from beating me. He beat my mother, too. Somehow he reasoned that she gave birth to me just to taunt him for screwing her sister.

I can tell you what it felt like when my mother's sister, my Aunt Mitzi , decided that the best Bar Mitzvah present she could give me when I was thirteen years old was my first piece of ass.

I can tell you about my first marriage. A happy one. And how I felt when I saw my twenty-five-year old wife, Sylvia, die, slowly from cancer.

I can tell you about my present marriage, and my wife, Theresa, who was determined to hold our marriage together. And, our daughter who had to live with the whole mess.

I can tell you how it feels to share a prison cell with a killer. What it's like to be locked up sixteen hours a day with this man who murdered another man with his bare hands. This man, Gordon Kirkwood-Yates, serving time for taking a life, sharing a cell with me, who never held a weapon against anyone. It's not uncommon in prison.

I can tell you how it feels to get thrown into a madhouse with a thousand other men who get the crazies, individually or collectively. I can tell you how it feels to be in the same prison with Charles Manson. And I can tell you why prisons don't work. What's it like to live where riots and bloodbaths are an everyday way of life. I know. Along with a thousand others, I lived it. The reason I know why a man would climb a prison wall knowing he'll be shot down, is because one such man was my friend.

And I'll tell you about the night I decided to change the course of my life. Not rehabilitate. CHANGE.

So, you look at the title and you ask me what the hell all this has to do with *The Call of the Cricket.* I'll tell you about that too.

Irwin Altman
San Francisco

I

Zayda died on my fifteenth birthday. I'm sure. Clearly. See: I'd spent the early morning hours that day in a Jackson, Mississippi, horror called a drunk tank. They locked me in with a pack of derelicts, winos, older guys. And I was frightened. No. I hadn't been drinking. I was hitchhiking through. Working my way from Los Angeles to New York City to stay with Zayda. I'd run away from home. I was frightened. Had good reason to be. I'd never been in jail or trouble before. Strangers all around me. Mother in Los Angeles; Zayda, my grandfather, in New York City; me, in Jackson, Mississippi, in jail.

Before and during World War II the South was really a foreign sight for a Yankee kid who'd never heard the word *nigger* except in hushed tones, behind closed doors. But in the South they're proud and loud in their opinions. And some of those opinionated people backed up their opinions with blackjacks, tar and feathers, flaming crosses, castration, rape, and other atrocities.

So, I was in jail with some of these loud clods, and as far as I was concerned in a foreign country as well. Derelicts, winos, urine and vomit and cockroaches all running rampant. And I was depressed over not knowing when they'd let me out and feeling dejected at the thought of spending my birthday lying on a concrete floor in jail. And I remembered the birthday cakes Aunt Mitzi baked for me.

When I was fifteen I wasn't aware of anything except my own raw feelings. And I had no defenses to keep me from crying. So, I did. Anti-Semitic slurs were not new to me, and I'd heard them before, out of the parroting mouths of kids in grade school: "Ike the kike . . . a good Jew's a dead Jew . . . Hitler is God's secret agent . . . Jews got all da money." Now I was hearing it again. Only the voices were meaner, more hostile, menacing; and I was hearing it in jail where I couldn't walk away from it. One wino in DT's screamed all night: "It weren't me . . . it were my Jew-boss sucked that nigger's prick!" And how could I forget one haggard old bastard who'd sworn "by Gawd" that he was going to see my behind. "Nuth'n like a ni-i-ce clean kid I alus say," he'd wheeze, grabbing his crotch and jacking the lump in his hand up and down. He never made a move toward me. But his snake-like presence kept me on edge. If he decided to spring on me, I knew that none of the other men lying half-stupored around the tank would have stood up to help me. And I had a feeling if I yelled for help they might have killed me. To them I wasn't a fifteen-year-old runaway. I was a "Gawdamn Yankee niggerluvva!"

It's hard enough being a fifteen-year-old in jail anywhere. But a fifteen-year-old kid locked in jail in the South is far worse.

Aside from constant talk about raping me I was treated to such outrageous advice by the more compassionate men such as, "Hit a nigger on da haid widda hamma—'sides he cain't feel it nohow . . . effen y'all wants good luck rubba nigger's kinky hair . . . effen y'all wanna change y'all's luck, fuck a niggerwoman—jes' pull her paints down rot whair she stands, boy, tain't rape effen it's a niggerwoman . . . the Jews hung dear Jesus on de cross . . . Jew-boys fuck thair mammys . . . Jew-boys are mammy fuckers."

I just took it. I crouched in a corner and took it. I could have said that Jewish boys don't do that to their mothers but I wasn't smart enough to handle those fellows—or strong enough and I didn't want to admit that I was Jewish. Besides, I was going through a trip about Aunt Mitzi. By then, I'd begun to wonder if my mother expected me to screw her, be a "mammy fucker," and if she knew that I had screwed Aunt Mitzi— her sister.

I didn't know that the jail officials had contacted my mother until the third morning, when one of the jailers appeared in front of the drunk tank. I remember he was a very fat man. And his head was shaved clean. And his eyes squinted as he called my name.

"Yes, sir," I said aloud as I pressed my face against the bars. He didn't say anything. Just gave me a sweeping look with his squinting eyes. Then, being satisfied it was me he wanted, he unlocked the cell door, and motioned me out saying, "We're kickin' y'all out, son. Reckon y'all are clean. Yore Mama sent y'all five dollahs. Follow me. We're gonna get y'all a b-i-ig breakfast at the restaurant next doah to heah—oniest place I kin fit inta a table. Oh, heah's a telegram come wit da money."

The telegram said: Sending five dollars. Don't come back. No room. Grandpa passed away two a.m. this morning. Go see Aunt Mitzi in New York. Happy birthday. Mother.

Zayda dead! Now what will I do, I worried . . . Aunt Mitzi, God I love her . . . What would Aunt Mitzi say if she knew that one of the men I'd been locked up with wanted to pull my pants off . . . Zayda dead! At the restaurant the jailer said to me, "Sorry 'bout yo' gran-pa, son. Reckon he's wit Jesus in heaven." I felt the urge to tell him that Jewish people don't worship Jesus. But I thought better of it. So I just said, "Yes sir," wondering if he would have offered his sympathy if I were black. Probably not, I thought.

"Listen, son," said the jailer, "this town ain't no place fo' a boy wit' no kinfolk. Ain't no work or nuthin' no how. An' all yo' poor mammy could send y'all was this here five dollars." He handed me the money order.

"Thank you, sir." I said, not knowing where I was going to get the money order cashed. But I wanted to get going without further delay.

"Now y'all know y'cain't hitchhike none round heah. Fact not hardly anywhair close. So what we gonna do, boy?"

"Well," I stammered. "I'll get on a bus east as soon as I get my check cashed. I'll get out, sir, don't worry." I searched his face for any hint of expression. Nothing but squinting eyes.

"No matta, I got a way figgered ta get y'all to New Yawk. Wanna hear it?"

What choice did I have? It was true, no hitchhiking. If I tried it, I'd get locked up again. So I listened to him tell me about a trucker friend of his. "Seems as though mah friend's got a full load of furniture to New Yawk. An' I know effen I ask him, he'll take y'all on as a lumper—y'all know, help carry furniture. He'll get yo' meals, an' a place ta stay on the way. He's kin ta the highway patrol man arrested y'all. See, we figger y'all got off wrong. Betta git back to y'all's kin. Yeah, yo' mamma mus' be mighty pore."

I wanted to tell him my mother had finally married very well after three months. Three months after my father died. I wanted to tell him what happened to father's gold chain watch and ruby ring, the only things father left after he died. Mother called her father in New York and said I had stolen the watch and the ring. When in fact I was not even able to go into my father's room when he was dying. And I couldn't understand why she had lied.

And I wanted to tell the jailer how after my father had been buried only a week my mother went out on her first date. And how I felt when mother patted me on the shoulder explaining to her new friend, the man she dated, "This is Irwin, my nephew from New York. My sister's divorced from her husband, so she sent Irwin out here til she got herself lined up again." Then mother would wink. The kind of wink that says: "I know you understand everything behind my winking eye, so no need to say a word in front of the kid here." So now I was my mother's nephew.

Sitting in that cafe with the jailer who'd found the time to be kind for a while I felt as though I should say something. I even felt as though I should apologize for mother, and for my being in Jackson, Mississippi. But how could I explain? How does a child's mind explain feelings he himself does not understand? How? How could I ask a stranger why my mother lied to her men friends? Even if I had taken the watch and the ring it was something my father had promised me and it was in the family. And up until the time my mother called me nephew I thought I had a family. But I did not take the watch and ring.

And why couldn't she tell them that I'd quit school when father died? That I went to work as a busboy at Thrifty's on Crenshaw for seventy-five cents a hour just to help mother and I survive (I really felt needed and important). And three weeks after father died when mother started to date heavily, why didn't she tell them, those men, that she could date, but she also had to spend some time with her son? But instead, while I was working as a busboy sometimes until late in the evening, she told them that I was running around, had no idea where I was and so she might just as well stay out.

During World War II it was hard as hell for a young woman like mother to find male companionship. Almost all the young male energy was being spilled on battlefields. So if the women wanted companionship they had to settle for young boys, old men. Mother had her share of both. And used to bring sailors and soldiers home to our little furnished room that we had taken after father died. I can still recall the sounds of her laughing, giggling and heated sex play. Our room was divided by a flimsy curtain that separated my bed from hers.

Well, it could have been worse. She could have killed me. But people don't necessarily have to die to be dead. And I believe I died when I became my mother's nephew.

Now that Zayda was dead, and I wasn't so certain about my future in New York, I felt like asking the jailer who'd been so kind to me if he'd like to have me for a son. But I didn't. I wanted to tell him that all these things happened—father dying, my being accused of stealing his jewelry, mother dating, my quitting school and going to work—just three weeks after we arrived in California. I never wanted to be with my father in the first place. Zayda was the only father I'd known until my father came back to claim mother and I when I was ten years old.

See: Mother was the first of her sisters to marry. A mistake. Because my father, a heavy gambler and self-appointed connoisseur of women, decided soon after I was born that screwing and playing cards was more desirable than a nagging wife and a kid that peed all over him. So, without a word, when I was three months old he disappeared. Mother and I moved into Zayda's house. We didn't hear from my father again until I was ten years old.

I wanted to tell the jailer that while strangers were crying at my father's funeral I sobbed in the basement of the funeral parlor. It seemed to me that I had just begun to get used to my father when he died. He didn't like me when I was fat, used to say to his friends, "Can't figure out how I got a fat kid like Irwin here." And after I'd lost all the weight because of the gland shots father said, "The gland shots cost a fortune. But if he didn't have them the kid would have never developed into a man. Would never have gotten hair or anything on his you- know-what. And what good's a man like that, hey fellas?"

But what my father failed to tell his friends was that it wasn't he who paid for the shots, it was Zayda. And what about that time father hit me in the face with his closed fist. Black eye. Bloody nose. Lump on my forehead. Had to tell the doctor I fell down a flight of stairs. I got that beating for being ten minutes late for dinner. I can remember saying, "I'm sorry, daddy, I'll never be late again. I promise." And, you know, I have never been late for anything since that day. Father never needed an excuse to beat my mother or myself. He seemed to blame my mother for my being so fat. Said he didn't believe I had an underactive pituitary gland—he thought I ate too much.

And at father's funeral when mother hadn't seen me cry because I'd been in the basement of the funeral parlor she said, "You must have ice water in your veins." But she said the same thing when I refused to get into bed with her. "I need to be comforted. You really are cold-blooded." Well, the thought repulsed me, and I did freeze. So, I thought perhaps I was cold-blooded.

I wanted to tell the jailer that the same month that mother remarried, I'd changed jobs. I'd gotten a better job. A junior stock clerk/shoe salesman at Berland's, a ladies' shoe store on Broadway in Los Angeles. And I'd turned over my whole paycheck to her. In a pawn shop I found a secondhand suit and a shirt and a tie that I needed for work. I can still remember that tie. It was one of those hand-painted jobs and smelled as though someone had wrapped fish in it. But it was okay because I never let anyone get close enough to smell it. And since I wanted mother to have the money I didn't want to buy another tie.

I enjoyed my job in the shoe store. It was fun. Hard work, fitting small shoes on big feet. But it had its compensations, at least I considered them compensations, because once in a while, while fitting an attractive woman for shoes I got to see all the way up her dress.

I always looked older than my age, at least after I began the gland shots. And one day, a girl with an exciting pair of legs asked me if I wanted to go to a movie. She even let me look up her dress—knowing it—while I was fitting her with shoes. Shoes were rationed during the war. I gave her my own ration stamps and said I'd meet her Saturday night. Payday was Friday. And instead of giving mother all my paycheck I held back enough money for a movie and ice cream and a new tie. Saturday morning mother said, "I had to borrow the money in your billfold last night." And she didn't even offer to explain why. So I took an advance against my pay. It was a great movie. A great date. We sat in the balcony and she even let me put my hand down the top of her dress. That in itself was worth the ration stamps, and helped me forget that my mother had taken money from me without asking.

I wanted to tell the jailer that I ran away from mother and her new husband when I saw my father's ruby ring. It was on her new man's hand. And he was wearing the gold watch on his vest. It wasn't the ring itself. Not the ruby. Not the gold. What the hell does a fifteen-year-old kid know about the real material value of metal and stone. And it wasn't because I loved my father. Any feelings I may have had for father faded along with the last black eye he'd given me.

But I guess I wanted the ring and watch so that I could lie to myself and say that he'd left them for me because he cared about me. When I told mother that I felt the ring should be mine, and that I also felt she should call Zayda and tell him that she had lied to him when she said I stole the jewelry, her only answer was, "Shame on you. Trying to put mother in a bad light. You know I wouldn't have said such a thing unless I was upset over your poor father's death. I really didn't know what I was saying, I was in such a state of shock. And now I can see that you really are incorrigible, the idea of you, my own son, wanting to make me look bad and not wanting your new father to have that nice jewelry." Well, maybe I'd have given him the ring. All on my own. I'll never know.

I wanted to tell the jailer that I ran away from home to go back to Zayda's house. And now I was worried, didn't know what to do, because Zayda was dead.

I wanted to tell the jailer that sitting in that cafe with him made me feel very important. Him being kind of an official and all and everyone there saying hello and asking and wondering who I was. "Oh, jes' a good friend of mine," the jailer said to them. I wanted to tell him everything. But I didn't. And I remember I wanted to cry. But I didn't. No. I didn't talk. I didn't cry. I just let things happen. And before the sun dipped into the Mississippi I had new friends, a set of work clothes, and a job as a lumper on the furniture van belonging to the jailer's friend. I can remember feeling important, again, for the first time since I left Zayda's house in New York.

I felt excitement. New York. Aunt Mitzi, mother's sister. It would be so good to see her and wouldn't she be surprised if I bought her a pair of silk stockings, which were scarce because of rationing. And maybe. Just maybe, she'd let me lie close to her—just like we'd done before. God, I missed Mitzi. Maybe I wouldn't tell her about my being in jail. Although mother might have. Maybe, I would just say to Mitzi, now that mother's married again, and has someone to take care of her, I've decided to be on my own. Work part-time. Go back to school. Become a writer like Sholem Asch, or a poet like Carl Sandburg, or a famous actor like Paul Muni, maybe. I remembered Mitzi was really crazy about Paul Muni. She told me that Paul Muni's real name was Muni Weisenfreund.

And that someday maybe I could be a great actor just like him. And I wanted to please Aunt Mitzi.

The trip on the van back to New York is mostly blurred in my memory. But I do recall a truck stop. A trucker's bunkhouse, and feeling mighty important being identified as one of the guys who belonged in that exciting on-the-road life. Traveling, always going some place, seeing the sights, the lights of the cities, and the amazing shapes and colors of nature, exchanging talk—grown-up man talk—with other truckers and their helpers about road conditions, scales, and even women. It amazed me that just one woman could be known by so many different men going and coming from just as many different directions. And I remember the truckers telling dirty jokes and laughing heartily.

And, I remember going out back of the bunkhouse to be alone so that I could cry for the wanting of a mother. Not mine. A new one. A mother who would appreciate a son who worked on the road and brought home the pay.

Then, my thoughts turned to Zayda. He was dead. My father was dead. And I said to myself, "Mother is dead."

Then my thoughts turned to Mitzi. Mother said I should go there. From the moment father deserted us and mother and I moved into Zayda's house in the Bronx, each of mother's sisters along with Zayda took part in my up-bringing. But from the moment I let go of the sides of my playpen and toddled across grandfather's living room floor, Mitzi was there. To catch my fall. Encourage me. Kiss my tears. And her cool fingers would trace smiles around my frowning face. Mitzi was warm laughter. Mitzi was gentle smiles. Mitzi was the maker of perfect, colorful jello molds, birthday cakes, sugarcoated orange peels and halavah. Mitzi was also trips to Coney Island. Fun days in the Bronx Park Zoo. You know, I remember one day while at the Bronx Park Zoo with Mitzi, holding on tight to her hand I took special notice of the strutting peacocks fanning their colorful feathers. Seeing all those colors on the peacocks reminded me of the way my mother put colors on her face in front of the mirror. And from that moment I wished that Mitzi was mother.

Mitzi gave me books to read. Including science fiction which she herself loved. And I can remember her saying that some day these stories will no longer be fiction.

About all I recall besides some of my thoughts out there in that field that night behind the bunkhouse are the smells of diesel fuel mingling with the night air. And I noticed there were fireflies. And remember wondering why fireflies glow—I knew—but I just wondered why . . . and then I heard the crickets singing into the night . . . and I wondered why crickets don't glow like fireflies. I wondered why people go to jail. I knew the men in that jail in Jackson were poor because they were scraping cigarette butts off the floor. And I remembered the jailer saying, "Once you go to jail you never stop going."

I don't know how long I stayed in that field alone with my thoughts. But I know it must have been late because almost all of the lights in the bunkhouse had gone out. I could no longer see the fireflies. And I could only hear one lonely cricket singing. And as I walked back to the bunkhouse I listened to the call of the cricket. I remember.

II

My horrid experience of having been in jail for the first time was now like a vivid memory of a bad dream. And the trip to New York on the furniture van had come to an end at a truck terminal in Manhattan. I can recall the excitement building in me as I walked toward the subway. I had twelve dollars from the money I'd earned as a lumper, and I still had the five-dollar money order Mother had sent me. And a paystub from a busboy job I took in Tucson, Arizona. My first job on the road. And I carried the small secondhand suitcase, that held some clothing I'd been able to buy along with three pair of silk stockings for Aunt Mitzi.

Though fall chilled the air I felt warm walking the streets of Manhattan again. The flickering signs, the lights dancing around, the civilians and servicemen home on leave, their girls holding on to their arms and laughing, being happy, rushing around, in and out of the stores and restaurants and theaters. Everything felt so alive. So vital. And after Father's death, Zayda's death, and my being in jail, the activity of the city braced me. I imagined that everyone noticed me, knew I'd been gone. And were nodding "Hellos" to me. And as I reached the entrance to the subway, I felt another surge of excitement. Now I was going to see Mitzi. And won't she be surprised to get the stockings!

There would be time afterward to go to Zayda's house. Mitzi: dark hair straying in shaggy wisps just above her firegreen eyes—eyes that were at times shaded by a fragile frown, more like a faraway gaze. She'd told me once that was the look she got when thinking about the skies and the stars and the planets. "I just try to imagine, Irwin, the people in the rest of the universe and I wonder if out there somewhere on another planet there's an aunt and nephew that share as much as we do."

I was able to get a seat on the train all the way from Grand Central Station in Manhattan to the Prospect Avenue El in the South Bronx.

All the trip I kept trying to imagine the expression on Mitzi's face—how those green eyes would fire up when she saw the stockings. Would she, I hoped, be as surprised as the time I brought her that picture of Paul Muni. A still shot from the time he played Emile Zola. That was the night of the first time. I'd gone to visit Aunt Mitzi and Uncle Dave, and standing looking at Aunt Mitzi in the doorway to their apartment I could feel something was wrong.

"Uncle Dave? He went to live with a fan dancer in Manhattan." Aunt Mitzi told me. "I don't expect to see him anymore." She seemed really upset the night she told me about it. It was just a few days after my Bar Mitzvah—and I remember being surprised over the news of his leaving because I'd seen Uncle Dave and Aunt Mitzi at my Bar Mitzvah reception. They'd seemed happy—arm in arm and all that.

So I hugged her and told her how badly I felt for her.

"Is there anything I can do," I asked Mitzi.

"No," she said, not being able to conceal the shadow of sadness in her eyes.

"Well, I brought you this picture of Paul Muni. Look, from *Emile Zola.*"

"Irwin. You never forget a thing. Do you. You know how much I love Muni. He's a great artist. But come in. Don't stand in the doorway. C'mon. I've got some halavah I just made—fresh." She smiled. And the sad shadow vanished from her eyes. Then, she led me inside by the hand, and pushed the door closed.

I followed her into her neat living room, tossed the Muni picture onto the coffee table and was almost ready to make myself comfortable on the sofa, when she said, "C'mon into the kitchen and keep me company while I cut the halavah. How's Zayda and everyone?"

"Oh—okay—I guess. I don't get to see Zayda much since my father moved us over to Hewitt Place. He don't like us. He's always hitting Mother and me—at least he could have let us stay at Zayda's."

"He's still hitting, huh. I don't even pretend to understand that man. Ever since he came back—what is it—three years now?"

"Uh-huh. When Buba died."

I watched Mitzi take the dish of halavah from the ice box. She placed it on the counter and went looking through the silverware drawer for a knife. I loved watching Mitzi. Always so neat. Everything always exact—perfect. And even when she was upset or had pressing matters to think about she managed to be pleasant without appearing forced.

"Is this enough?" she asked, handing me a slice of halavah tucked in a napkin.

"For now. Sure looks good. Thanks."

"Don't go overboard on that stuff. Don't want to gain that weight back now. You look so handsome—all slimmed down. But, then," she teased, "you were always my special boyfriend—even when you gained all that weight. C'mon, let's go in the living room and talk. You didn't even notice the new painting I'm working on. I'll show you."

She was right. I hadn't noticed the "new painting," I guess because I'd become so accustomed to seeing Mitzi's easels, paints, and canvases around. Landscapes, character studies and so forth.

Following her into the living room, I spotted it right off. It was a nude woman—reclining on her side.

"I guess I didn't notice because I was facing the back of the canvas. Gee, that's really good. I wish I could paint like that or any way at all."

"Practice. Lots of it."

"I can just see my father and mother letting me paint naked women—Father doesn't let me paint or draw or anything like that."

"Nudes," Mitzi corrected. Then she laughed. "They may be naked. But in art they're nudes. Besides you were doing pretty good—even when you were ten years old—when I was teaching you."

It felt good—standing near Mitzi. Enjoying her painting—

just like when we were at Zayda's.

"Yeah. But remember when my father moved into Zayda's house? Right after Buba died—when you married Uncle Dave."

"Yes?"

"He made me put all my sketches in the basement—said a person couldn't earn a living that way. Then, when I told him I liked it—it was fun, and you were teaching me, he got angry—called you a name . . ."

"What kind of name? C'mon—let's sit on the sofa."

"I'd rather not say."

We sat on the sofa and Mitzi moved in close to me. She put her arm around me just like she'd done so often in the past, when I'd cuddle close to her and feel the whole world was right.

"Irwin, I thought you and I had a very special friendship. We could always talk about anything. You could even talk to me about girls—right?"

"Yes. But you know I don't like my father. And no matter what he says I just don't pay attention."

"Irwin," she insisted. "Come here closer—that's right. Now you know I love you. Ever since you were a baby—you were special to me. Now you know you can say anything to me—and I'll still love you."

"Well, my father called you a tramp," I said. Then, tried to move away from her. I was embarrassed. And I didn't want to hurt her.

"C'mere—you aren't going anywhere." She pulled me back to her. And I was not inclined to resist.

"Aunt Mitzi, I'm sorry. I apologize for my father," I said. But she didn't answer. Just held me close against her breasts. And I became aware of her breathing and her breasts rising and falling. Mitzi always had different ways of making me feel important. This was one of them. Our pretend game. Pretending I was her boyfriend. We would kiss—she showed me how to kiss a girl. But I never got a chance to try it out on anyone except Mitzi—not with the tongue and all.

Anyway, sitting close to her in silence for a long while, I'd already begun to forget Father, Mother, and whole world.

Finally she spoke. "Somehow your father will feel regret for the way he treats people. But never mind. There's more important things to talk about."

Then she put me at arms' distance and asked, "Did you get a lot of presents for your Bar Mitzvah?"

"Yeah, quite a lot. But mostly cash. About five hundred dollars. Father said he'd put it away for me."

"Oh no!" she gasped. "Well, I hope he doesn't decide to parlay it for you."

"What?"

"I mean, I hope he doesn't stop at the racetrack on the way to the bank . . . But I'm sure he wouldn't be that low—well, that's good. That's a good start now that you're almost officially a man."

"What do you mean 'almost officially?' "

"You'll see—soon—but remember Irwin, not money and not clothes makes a man. It's how you treat people. How you express yourself. It's not displaying muscles and . . ." She stopped abruptly.

"And what?"

More silence. She just looked at me as though trying to see through me.

"And what?" I asked again.

"Being brutal. But, of course, thanks to your Zayda—you know about that."

"Oh. I could never hit people, like my father does."

"Do you kiss girls?"

"No. At least not the way you showed me. Not yet. There's one, I'd like to. But I'm afraid to ask her."

"Who's that?"

"Angela."

"Thought so. She's a pretty girl. I'll bet she'd let you. But don't get carried away. Do you still remember how I taught you to kiss?"

"Oh, sure!" I said, trying to sound like a know-it-all adult.

"I imagine now that you've lost all that weight—the other problem is taken care of too? I notice your voice is getting deeper."

I knew what she meant by "other problem." She was getting around to wanting me to take my pants down—and I wanted to. But for some reason I felt shy. "Oh, that's not all," I said proudly. "I've even got hair on my chest."

"Oh! Let me see! It's been a few months since I've checked you over."

Feeling just a slight twinge of embarrassment, I moved close to her again and unbuttoned my shirt. I shouldn't have felt embarrassed with Mitzi. But I did. After all, she was my confidante. And she's bathed me so often. We even took baths together—and from the time I was almost twelve years old she kept a close concerned watch over my coming manhood—or lack of it, as was the case because of my underdeveloped pituitary. Let me tell you, I was one kid that had lots of attention paid to his prick. She'd say, "Just because I'm married and don't live with Zayda anymore doesn't change the fact that I am your aunt and you're my special boyfriend/nephew. So you just let me see what's going on with you—but not if your uncle is here. And just like everything else we share—it's our secret."

Our "sharing" had been our secret from the onset. It never occurred to me to tell. Even the time mother wanted me to "comfort" her—after father's death. I wanted to say, you know that by tradition a child can't do that with a parent. Aunt Mitzi already told me all about it. But it fits. If you lie you also break sacred traditions. But I remembered that "the child," according to Aunt Mitzi, "does not even talk about it with the parents."

"Not that the parents don't already know. They do. But it's just not talked about. Understand?"

I almost slipped and told mother about Mitzi and me that time she patted me on the shoulder while she lied to her man friend, "This is my nephew. . . ." I thought to myself: Boy, don't she wish! If I were her nephew she would have had to be the one to teach me about sex and how could I keep any "secret" with her? Mother had already told two lies about me—told Zayda I stole my father's ring and watch. And now this business about my being my own mother's nephew.

Poor Zayda! Father and Zayda had been enemies. They died less than a year apart . . . and now Zayda would not know the truth about the watch and ring. Thanks to mother's lies Zayda died believing I was a thief.

The first time Mitzi wanted to have a look at my prick was that day at Zayda's, when she caught me and Frankie and Philip in the wine cellar—de-pants-ing Harvey. I wasn't quite twelve. And by that time she'd been married and living a block away from Zayda's for two years. And I had been going to the doctor for shots three times a week for a year without any visible results. I was still fat. Still no signs of puberty. And the whole family was worried.

And during those two years my father had moved in and out of Zayda's a couple of times—always promising to come back. "Just as soon as I can get a place for us," he'd say. I hoped that day would never come because he always ridiculed me for being fat, and hit me and mother often.

I did meet some of father's family in that period. Aunts. Uncles. And cousins I never knew existed. They seemed nice enough. Far more pleasant than my father—but we never became close. All except for his sister Lillian who taught drama at the American Academy of Dramatic Arts. She insisted on teaching me "dramatic arts." "Someday you'll lose weight and be a leading man, and if you don't lose weight you can be a character actor—they get more work anyway."

Aunt Lillian even pushed me into a part on a kiddie radio show called "Rainbow House." It was over WOR radio and I liked doing radio. Bob Emery, the director, made a big noise about my soprano voice and I sang in the chorus along with taking parts that fit the voice—even female roles.

My father beat me because he couldn't cope with my being fat. He forced spinach down my stomach. "You gotta be like me," he say, flexing his muscles, "like, me and Popeye the Sailor. Your Zayda is one of those cockeyed socialists. Always with the high-sounding words. Listen kid. In this world it's who can shake the highest roll on the dice, wear the most expensive clothes, and punch the hardest."

"Yes, Father."

And when I took the dice from my Monopoly set and rolled them on the kitchen table he said, "Good. But let me show you a better way to handle those cubes."

So, he showed me how to hold the dice "professional." They'll get you further than your Zayda's socialist words. If I'd known he was feeding you all that stuff I'd've come for you sooner."

"Yes, Father."

"See this gold watch, even the chain is solid gold!"

"Yes, Father."

"My father's. Left it for me when he died. He was no different than your Zayda. And when we came over on the boat to America from Russia—it was right after my Bar Mitzvah—and I got out on those streets around Second Avenue still wearing my long sideburns and *yamalka* on my head it didn't take long for the American kids to jump me. Boy did they beat me up. Really tough."

"But I was lucky. I wasn't fat like you. I could handle myself. So I picked the leader of the gang, beat him up until he cried 'Uncle' and after that we all became friends."

"Yes, Father."

"And that acting stuff my sister is teaching you. Well, that's for the birds. It's okay for her. Being a woman. But not for you. Not if you're going to be my son."

"But I like acting. And Aunt Lillian and Bob Emery say I'm pretty good."

"Are you talking back to me?"

"No, Father. I'm sorry."

"Well, see that you don't. You gotta learn respect. I don't like hitting you all the time. Makes me feel bad. But I love you and I want you to learn respect and how to take a good licking. Pretty soon I'll show you how to give one. Okay?"

"Yes, Father."

"See this ruby ring—solid gold setting."

"Yes, Father."

"I won it. Pretty huh?"

"Won it?"

"Yeah. In a dice game. Tell you what. If you lose weight before I die, the ring and the watch are yours. I'll leave them for you. And you got to give up this silly radio acting too. They don't pay you anyway."

"No. Not right now. But I'm just learning with Bob Emery."

"I don't want an argument, kid. Besides I don't want you around all those faggots."

"Faggots?"

"Yeah. Probably Bob Emery's one of those fairy-boys."

"Fairy-boy. Like in a nursery rhyme?"

"Holy Joe. What's your Zayda been teaching you? A fairy's a man that—that loves another man. Got it?"

"You mean like I love Zayda or like you say you love me?" I asked. I didn't have the vaguest idea about what father was talking about.

"No," father snapped. "Not like that. When you get hair around your thing you'll know. You sure are taking a long time with that. I guess those shots aren't working too good."

"Father?"

"Yes."

"What'll happen if I don't get hair?"

"Well, you know about what men and women do when they're older—don't you?"

"Well, yes, I think so." Now, here was a chance to show father I wasn't as dumb about the world as he thought. "Harvey found some pictures of men and women doing it. Found them in an envelope on the sidewalk. Thought it was money or something. Anyway he showed us the pictures. But we'd been talking about those things anyway."

"You tell Harvey to bring those pictures here. Does his mother know he's got them?"

"No. He keeps them hid."

"I'll keep them for you boys. Safer that way."

"But they belong to Harvey." I worried. Harvey would have a hemorrhage when he finds out I told.

"I'll talk to Harvey myself. Never mind."

"But you didn't answer my question. About the hair."

"Well. If you don't get hair you won't be able to do what the men and women in those pictures were doing. Get it?"

But, when I reached twelve-and-a-half years old the shots began to take effect and I was going to be able to do it like in Harvey's pictures (which my father never returned).

And when I was twelve-and-a-half I was out of radio acting. Short career.

So, at age thirteen I knew that daisies and sunflowers and roses and pictures of Paul Muni and Buba's blintzes and Zayda's garden and sharing baths and directing anger without violence and laughing and singing and hugging and kissing and constantly striving for the highest possible good was more desirable than my father's beatings and my mother's detachment from the world.

I was aware of higher order. But I found out that that awareness put me in a minority group.

And when father made his promise good and took mother and I from the cloister of Zayda's home, I found myself on the battlefield of the majority. When people spit at me, I didn't know how to spit back. And I didn't know a damned thing about alternatives.

I was a fat kid in a skinny world. A world where men were paid by the inch from the ground up and according to the depth in the cleft of the chin and according to the lengths of their pricks. And a woman's worth was measured by the size of her boobs and buttocks and her prick-sucking techniques. And a world where guns spit authority.

So, by the time the day arrived when I brought Muni's photo to Aunt Mitzi, a multitude of changes had occurred in my life. But the three years, from age ten to age thirteen, the changes poured over me like molten lava.

Buba's, my grandmother's, death—my first experience

with death—was a frightening experience for me.

As late as the nineteen-thirties, orthodox Jews did not embalm their deceased. And Buba's body remained in the house. She lay at rest in a casket that was placed in the center of the dining room—on the dining room table. She remained there midst the family's hysterical crying, crying friends coming to pay respect, and morticians coming twice a day to bathe her.

No one had ever spoken to me about death other than saying, "We die and go to heaven if we're good and hell if we're bad." And whoever it was that said it had a fanciful description of both heaven and hell. But until Buba died when I was ten years old I'd never touched death—its cold reality. So, I believe I thought Buba was only very ill and the bathing applied by the morticians would cause her to get well, and get up and walk. Smile. Sing. And tell fortunes to the friends who were crying over the casket, and fry *blintzes*, and take a puff from Zayda's cigarette, and tell me stories about her childhood in Rumania—and comb my hair, and rub my back, and nurse me on her warm loving breasts.

But when I saw the morticians stuff cotton batting into her mouth and stitch her gums together with wire and when I saw the morticians take a large safety pin and stick it through her breasts so they would keep from falling over her side, dress her, paint her cheeks with rouge, smear her lips, those lips that kissed my tears, those lips that held hemming pins when she altered our clothes, those loving lips that kissed us "a kiss for children," those loving lips that kissed Zayda "a kiss for husband when we were orphan children in Rumania and still thought we were sister and brother we kissed on da cheek. Oy, vat ve missed. Huh, Papa?"

It wasn't until the lid on her pine casket was closed and screwed down tight, I became hysterically aware of death. I screamed, "Open the box—open it!" And I couldn't believe that when I picked daisies and sunflowers from the garden— special for Buba—I would never again hear her voice say, "So beautiful, so beautiful—and did you tank de earth for the flowers?" I ran over to Zayda, screaming. Hot tears ran down my cheeks. Kicking Zayda in the shins I screamed again, "Make them open the box, Zayda—make them!"

"Anyway, Irwin," Aunt Mitzi said, "I think that hair on your chest is beautiful. Because now it won't be any problem to do what an aunt is supposed to do for her nephew the week of his Bar Mitzvah."

Mitzi's voice sounded huskier than usual. Her breathing became heavy. And I sensed something different was about to happen. And she noticed me shaking. "Since when have you ever been afraid of me, Irwin?" she asked gently, but still sounding heavy.

"Not ever, Aunt Mitzi. And it's not you I'm afraid of. I don't know what it is that's making me shake."

Mitzi hugged me tightly for a moment. "Remember how I'd hug you when you were a little boy. It always made you feel good. Maybe this will help you stop shaking."

"It's not working. I'm still shaking. Maybe I'd better go for a walk and come back later."

She moved away from me asking, "Want some more halavah?"

"No, please don't go in the kitchen. I've got something to ask you," I answered. "And it's not easy."

"Of all people. If you can't ask me—I don't know who else it would be. So, try. Won't you?"

"Well, remember those games you and I used to play in the bathtub at Zayda's?"

"Yes, I do. Button, button, who's got the button that was fun—reaching down in the water looking for buttons."

"Well, a few nights ago, while I was bathing, washing around—well, you know . . ."

"You mean washing down there?" she said pointing to my fly.

"Yeah. Down there." I said, shivering. "Well, I got to thinking about how we played "button, button" and I was pretending that you were looking for the button like you always did . . . and . . . I . . . and . . ."

"Did your thing get hard?"

"Y-yeth. And I c-couldn't stop."

"So marvelous, Irwin. I'm so happy for you. And what you did many people do—men and women."

"W-well, my f-father once asked me if I ever did that. He said that it makes you c-crazy."

"Well, Irwin, that's not so. The only thing is, if you do it to yourself too much you may find it too pleasurable and then it would be difficult for a woman to please you. But otherwise—especially at your age—when it's hard to find a girl who knows what to do—or even do it at all—it's alright. Nothing wrong with it.

"Y'know, I remember the last time I checked you over I thought I saw the start of something, but I didn't say anything. Wanted to be sure, I guess."

I calmed down a bit but I recall being shaky. "Mitzi, there's something else you should know."

"Yes, sweetheart?" her eyes reflected misty joy.

"Well, remember how we always talked about going away in a spaceship. Just the two of us?"

"I remember."

"Well, that's what I thought about when that happened in the bathtub."

"I'm flattered. That makes me happy. Were we playing button, button in your spaceship?"

"Y-yeth. But no bathtub. I wasn't going to tell you any of this. I wasn't going to come to see you either."

"Why not? You know how much your problem has worried me. Now I feel better. Why wouldn't you want to tell me?"

"Because I was afraid you'd ask to see the rest of me after I showed you the hair on my chest."

"Irwin! After all these years do I detect a little shyness about bodies?"

"But I'm afraid if I show you it would stand up again."

"Why, that's beautiful. I've been waiting a long time for this very moment. But if you don't feel you can show me just yet—it can wait till another time."

I had no such intention as to wait. I was just nervous. That's all. Mitzi was wearing the white pleated skirt and green blouse I liked so well on her. I enjoyed looking at Mitzi and even though I'd seen her without clothes so often—I had lately begun to peek up her skirt whenever I could. And the way the pleated skirt flared when she crossed her shapely legs made looking easier. Fascinating, what stockings will do for a woman's legs. "But it's different now. I get strange feelings."

"Irwin. I want you to listen for a moment. By our traditions an aunt is supposed to teach the nephew—everything. Everyone knows. But no one speaks of it. Not ever. You don't tell mother, father, grandparents, friends—anyone. To break the silence breaks tradition. And sons don't do it with mothers or daughters with fathers. It is written in a secret book. Only for the eyes of our women. And it is not as though we were just any ordinary aunt and nephew. I've practically raised you."

"Secret books?" I replied. My knees went rubbery. But I'd learned to have respect for books. "It is written," Zayda would say. And I'd learned that according to Jewish tradition, if "It is written," it's law. So if the book said the aunt takes care of the erection that was okay with me.

"Secret," smiled Mitzi, putting both arms around my neck. "It won't hurt. I will see to it that it is the highest possible pleasure for you."

"But I don't know how to . . . the guys and I only talk about it."

"I know for the two of us," she interrupted. Then, taking her arms away from around my neck she reached for my hand. "Come into my bedroom." I stretched out on the bed. And I felt frightened. Nervous. And flushed with excitement. Then Mitzi sat down on the edge of the bed facing. Placing her hand on my thigh she said, "Now, darling, this is the first step."

She moved her hand upward and unzipped my fly. Then undid my pants. Then my belt. She put her hand inside my fly saying, "You feel so beautiful."

Ever since I was a small child Mitzi had fooled around with my prick. And it was enjoyable fun and games. But now I was enjoying it in another way. A brand new game. I liked it.

"Here," she said, "move over a bit so I can lay close to you. Then you can touch me too."

Once beside me, she took my hand and guided it all the way up her dress and I could feel the soft hair through her pants, her warmth. I began to tremble harder and I remembered the days when she'd guide my hand between her legs to help me "find the button." I didn't tremble then. But, now. Oh yes.

And this time, when my hand reached the place she wanted, she said, "Oh, my darling, secret boyfriend, I've waited so long for you. Now I will show you how to love a woman and how a woman should make you feel."

"Mitzi."

"Yes, my little sweetheart."

"I'm scared."

"Soon, you won't be. Tell you what. I'll lay perfectly still and you unbutton my blouse. Lift my skirt if you want. I've seen you peeking. Now you can look. All you want."

And in the moments that followed we'd undressed each other, kissed each other and she held my head to her breast so I could press my lips to her firm nipples.

"Irwin, am I your favorite person?" she asked.

"Yes. You know that."

"And will you keep our secret?"

"Of course."

"Then, wait no longer, slide over on top of me—and I will help you inside me—where you belong."

And feeling the new, exciting experience her moist warmth surrounding me, I felt as though I did belong. After all, it is written.

"So," Mitzi said, "now you know. Now, you've stopped shaking. And I am delighted in your presence. Happy thirteenth birthday, today you are a man." Well, if a piece of ass makes you a man, I was a man. And I liked it. "And the Lord made the light and saw that it was good . . ."

"Mitzi."

"Yes, little lover?"

"I don't want to go home. I want to be here with you. I hate my father. And mother doesn't care about me."

"Oh, Irwin. You flatter me so much. But, it just can't be that way. You can come back as often as you like. Every day if you want. But to move in with me it would make problems. This way we can do this often. Come, let's take a bath—just like we always have—huh. I'll teach you a new game. It's called docking the spaceship. Then you have to get dressed and go home. It's getting late."

"Okay," I said, reluctantly, "but I'd rather stay here."

"Oh, you like my halavah?" she laughed.

"Not as much as I like you."

"Next time you're here, I'll show you that halavah is not the only food for the soul."

And that's how it was for the next two years. Mitzi taught me everything sexual. After which my father took mother and I to California.

Now, I was back. And as I rang the door bell to Mitzi's apartment, a surge of excitement and eager anticipation took my breath.

III

Sitting on the couch next to Mitzi again I felt as though I were home. She opened the package. "Oh, silk stockings! How marvelous! How did you ever manage to get these. And the right size, too." She kissed me on the cheek. Not the kind of kiss I expected.

"I just took a chance. I'm glad you like them." I said, waiting to see if she'd kiss me again. But she didn't.

"I do. They're so hard to get, what with silk being used for parachutes and all. This war business is terrible."

"If I were old enough I'd join the Navy," I said feeling a slight guilt.

"It's just as well you're not of age. I don't know what I'd do if anything happened to you. Buba gone. Zayda gone. Your father gone."

I detected a noticeable but a brief change—a catch—in Mitzi's voice when she said "father gone," but I didn't inquire. I just said, "mother's married again."

"Yes, I know. It seems as though she couldn't wait."

"They had a champagne party for her wedding. They made me go."

"Made you go—why?"

"Well, they said, 'It's only proper.'"

"Proper, my behind. Well, never mind. It's late. You must be tired. Do you want to stay here tonight? Then tomorrow we can go over to Zayda's house."

"I don't know if I want to see the house right now. Who's staying there—Aunt Annie?"

"Yes, she's taking care of details. There's been a lot of confusion since Zayda died last month. Money and property. A big mess. But I'll tell you about it tomorrow. There's time. Would you like something to eat before you go to sleep?"

Mitzi was avoiding conversation. Not like her. And I was wondering why she'd only kissed me on the cheek when I gave her the stockings. Not like it was before. Something was wrong. Maybe Zayda's death. That could be it. I know I was upset by it. I really didn't want to see the house again. Just wanted to be with Mitzi. "No, I'm not hungry. Just tired. And I need a bath."

"Sure. I'll get you a clean towel and washcloth." She got up and headed for the linen closet in the hallway. "Oh, by the way, do you want to see the letter I got from your mother?"

"Mother?" I panicked. Now I knew why Mitzi was cool to me. She knew I'd been in jail. Mother told her. "Uh . . . no, not now. What did she say?"

"Oh, just that she'd appreciate it if I'd let you sleep on the couch for a few days and that you'd been picked up in Mississippi and put in jail."

She knew! "Well, I was hitchhiking. It's against the law." I held my breath wondering what her response would be.

"I hope they didn't treat you too badly," she said.

I got up, walked into the hallway and stood close to her. "It was pretty terrible—awful! But they knew I didn't commit any real crime and the jailer there got me a job on a truck with a friend of his. I worked my way. All the way. I even had a job in a restaurant in Tucson, Arizona. A busboy. Look. I saved this paystub. I was going to look for a job in Mississippi and try to get enough money saved to take a bus. And if I didn't get arrested I would have. I was broke— almost. But a few people that gave me rides bought me some meals. I sure got dirty on the road. And the jail was dirty. Terrible!

"But, now I know how to be a lumper on a truck" That said, I thought Mitzi would be impressed. But she didn't respond.

"Here's a towel (if you don't mind using the washcloth on the tub)—I don't have any clean washcloths. Gotta do some laundry," she said. Her mind seemed to be elsewhere. And she seemed disturbed. I began to feel as though I were in the way. And I didn't take the towel.

"Aunt Mitzi," I said apologetically. "I have a few dollars and if I'm in the way I could get a room somewhere."

Suddenly Mitzi dropped the towel wrapped her arms

around me and burst into heaving tears. She was so upset. I'd never seen her that way. And the only way I knew to deal with it was to put my arms around her and hold her tightly. I remember stroking her head, but I said nothing. I only hurt for her. After a few minutes she calmed down. Enough to smile weakly. "Oh," she sobbed trying to regain control of herself. "Look how you've grown—you're as tall as I am—I've hardly noticed I've been in such a turmoil. And I am happy to see you. What makes you think you're in the way? My God, Irwin, I've been worried sick about you. Your mother should be ashamed. I have a thing or two to tell that sister of mine."

Relieved, and overjoyed knowing Mitzi wanted me there, I joined her tears with my own. And there we stood in each other's arms sharing tears of grief mingled with the joy of being together.

"Look at us," said Mitzi, "standing here, crying. We should be thankful to be together."

"I did miss you, Aunt Mitzi. And I thought about you all the time. I wish we'd never gone to California."

"Well, you're here now. And we've lots to talk about. Lots. But first take your bath. What's in your suitcase? Do you have clean underwear and socks? What about a pair of pajamas?"

"Everything but pajamas. I've been sleeping in my shorts lately."

"Your mother says, 'Sleep on the couch . . .' is that what you want to do?"

"No. I'd much rather sleep in your bed."

"Oh. And I sleep on the couch. Right?"

"Mitzi?"

"Yes, Irwin. What is it? Tell me."

"Can we both sleep in your bed?"

She was hesitant for a moment. Then she moved close to me, pressing firmly against my groin.

"Yes, I think we should—for tonight anyway. And tomorrow? Who knows. No one can count on tomorrow. And no one should live in yesterday's shadow. Go get your bath. I'll come in and wash your back," she said, all the while rubbing against my groin.

Releasing my hold from around her back I let my hands reach around her bottom and I pulled her closer.

"Oh," she said, "I see you haven't forgotten your lessons. Been practicing?"

"No. No one to practice with." I didn't see any point to telling Mitzi about the one date when I put my hand down the front of that girl's dress. After all, it wasn't all the way, like being in bed or anything.

"Oh, that's too bad. Poor Irwin. Well, we've got some practicing to do—don't we?"

Evening blended into early morning. Rain sprinkled down the bedroom window. Mitzi and I were in bed touching shoulders, talking the morning away.

"We should try to get some sleep, but I've missed you so much it's just good to hear your voice—be close . . . And there is something I must tell you; I am trying to work up the courage."

"Since when do we need courage to talk to each other?"

"Well, dear, sweet, darling nephew, this is not a thing easily explained."

"I had something to talk to you about too. Would it be easier if I said mine first?"

"Maybe. I don't know. No. It won't make it easier. Maybe just possible. Tell me. What's on your mind?"

"You. You're on my mind."

"How? In what way."

"Well, see. I'm really a man now. I mean *really*. I'm fifteen. Be sixteen next month. And I'd like to stay here in New York with you. Get a job. Give you my pay for food and clothes and everything—we could even go to the movies sometimes."

At this, she scooted away from my side and sat up straight in bed. She was almost speechless. All she could do was stammer. "But . . . But . . ."

"Let me finish." I said not giving her a chance to put her words together. "Oh, I know we're not husband and wife and all that stuff. Maybe someday you'll get another husband. But right now we could be together. I just don't want to go back to Mother."

A long silence followed. She sat almost motionless. Then she scooted back flat on the bed closer to me than before. "Irwin, you are priceless," she said sliding her arm through mine. "Offering me your pay. God, your Zayda really taught you. You're not like your father . . . sorry . . . you're not like a lot of men I could think of. In fact, I didn't tell you, but until just last week I've been working at the Horn and Hardart Automat. But I got fired."

"Fired . . . Why?"

"Oh, an old man knocked on a sandwich window I was filling, and he had such a hungry look. So I just released the catch on the coin lock, the little glass door flew open . . . I was gonna pay for the sandwich, I just wanted to feed the old man—but it turned out that someone reported me to the manager before I had a chance to go back to the locker room and get my purse—we're not allowed to carry money while working. So, I got fired. Didn't even give me a chance to explain."

"Well, you don't need that job. I can help you with money. Even right now. I've got almost twelve dollars in my pocket. Plus a five-dollar money order. And I'll go out tomorrow and get a job."

"Irwin," she pleaded, "stop it. You're only making it more difficult for me to say what I want to say. Besides Zayda—God rest his soul—loaned me a lot of money before he died. And money is not what I need. In fact, I'll give you some to help you get started."

Her tone of voice was high and tense. And I could sense a rejection. But I was afraid to jump to conclusions. So, I waited for her to continue. After what seemed a long silence she said, timidly, "It's all wrong, Irwin, the whole thing is wrong. And it's my fault. And when I tell you you'll hate me, but I hope not—because I love you."

My muscles drew up tight and I wondered what more could be wrong. "Don't be silly, Aunt Mitzi. I could never hate you. Nothing you could say could do that. Nothing. Don't forget that either."

She seemed not to hear my promise and she began to pull at her words as though she were trying to pull odds and ends from a trunk so she could close the lid—and lock it. For good.

"What I'm about to say to you hurts me—has hurt me— deeply for a long time. And I've always asked you to 'keep our secrets' and you have. But this one I hope will stay with you forever. Still, if it doesn't . . . if you can't keep it. I will understand. And still love you. I ask you only to try. Try hard."

Mitzi always had an air of mystery about her. Always the stories. And always the songs of the stars. Always taking me on mind trips to other planets . . . worlds that defied imagination. And she'd made them sound plausible. And she always put us in her stories. Her favorite was about the time—in another life—when she and I were rulers of the planet Lam: the invisible planet. Not even the most sophisticated telescopes in the universe could detect our planet, she'd say. Not because we were really invisible, but we were infinitesimal— so tiny not even a super-microscope could uncover it. Then she went on to explain that size was relative and that to us everything was just as though it is on this planet. Only more peaceful. More evolved. Millions of people and we ruled according to the wishes of the people. Not like politicians today. Give them a vote and they screw you. More like servants. But we were happy. "Someday, Irwin, I'll take you to the ocean by Coney Island and I'll point out the exact spot of our orbit. You gotta stand on the boardwalk between the steeplechase and the funhouse, but facing the ocean . . ."

When Buba died was the first time Mitzi told me that story. And with the passing years she added more details. But always saying, "Someday we'll go back there. We're only visiting Earth for a short while. Kind of a special mission."

So many times in prison Mitzi's stories would screw around my head. And in the crazies I'd think they had substance.

And it was no different the night I returned to New York from California. So much had gone wrong and I was looking for Mitzi to take me back home. Back to the planet Lam. But, though I wanted it to be real, I knew it wasn't. I was acutely aware of my own screwed-up life. And lying in bed with Mitzi, listening to her gentle voice I was almost afraid to hear what she had to say. Because while I had no idea what she had in mind I sensed I'd be looking for another place to live.

Earlier that evening she told me about an uncle I'd never known. A brother, Zayda's only son. "No one was allowed to speak of him, Irwin. Zayda said a *kaddish*—the prayer of mourning for the dead—for him, and according to tradition my brother was dead. He was the eldest of us kids. Ran off. Came back home with a wife. A *shicksa*, a gentile. Zayda banished him from the house and his life 'forever.' And mourned secretly for him ever since. But it was as though he never existed.

"Anyway, I guess Zayda must have been doing a lot of looking into himself and according to his last will and testament he recognized his son 'a child of God' and reinstated his status as older son. Left him every nickel. The house. Everything. And now he's supposed to take care of us girls financially. But I'll tell you something, Irwin. I don't believe he will. No. I don't believe it at all. Haven't heard from him since the will was read. Can't reach him either—that's what most of your mother's letter was about—Zayda's money. Probably, none of us will see a penny of it. Okay by me. But I'd give anything to sit in on the court battle. Your Zayda and Buba gave me more than money can buy."

Obviously Mitzi wasn't quite so disturbed over Zayda's money. But she was sure as shit in a tangle over what she wanted to talk to me about. And the longer she took getting to it the more inwardly upset I became. "I know what you're going to tell me," I said, finally. "There really is no such place as the planet Lam. Right?"

This brought a laugh and she said, "Oh, but there is, nephew, there is. Just as sure as there's a Santa Claus."

We both laughed. No matter what. There was, with Mitzi, always something to laugh about. And it never seemed vulgar or out of place. "Mitzi, please," I prodded, "please get it over with."

She took a deep breath and let it out saying, "We're not supposed to be doing what we do. We should not be in bed together. We should not be having sexual things together. Not now. Not before. Not ever. It's wrong—wrong!"

She drew a deep breath and sighed in relief and sat around on the edge of the bed completely away from me. I remained silent. I didn't want to let on that I'd figured that out for myself. And I didn't want to tell her that even if it was wrong I enjoyed being with her more than I did anyone. And I liked sex with her. Hell, I just loved sex. I never knew anyone but her sexually up to that time, but along with everything else in my life Mitzi made sex very beautiful.

"I don't understand, Mitzi, why is it wrong. It's so beautiful. So good."

"Blood relatives just are not supposed to do it with each other. It's not morally right. Socially right. Mentally right or any other kind of right. And I lied to you. There's no tradition about aunts and nephews, there's no secret book. And no matter what my reasons may have been—I was wrong. It can never be again. Not ever!"

Now she got up from the bed. Daylight peeked through the window shades and cast a pale halo around her slender curves. I felt angry and hurt. Not that she'd lied to me. No. Not that at all. But I had no where else to go. And I loved Mitzi deeply. She was sending me away.

"Mitzi."

She wouldn't look at me. "Yes, Irwin. What is it?"

"Will we ever go back to Lam?"

"Maybe. In another life."

"Can I stay here with you until I get a job?"

"You should go back to California. Go back to school. Get an education. I can buy you a bus ticket."

"I won't go back to mother. I love you. If I could, I'd marry you. And even if we can't be in bed together I'd like to stay for a little while."

"Look, get some sleep. It's six o'clock in the morning. I'll sleep on the couch. Later we'll talk about it. Okay."

"Mitzi."

"Yes."

"Would you kiss me goodnight?"

She came back to the bed. Kissed me on my forehead. And I knew that I would be leaving that day. I knew I would not go to Zayda's house. I knew I would not go back to mother. But I'd go out and get rich. Become an actor like Paul Muni—or a writer like Sholem Asch or a professional gambler like my father. And come back in a big shiny limousine with a chauffeur just like all the big rich people on Park Avenue. I'd come back for Mitzi. Escort her into the limousine. Have the chauffeur drive us to Coney Island, and we'll look for the planet Lam on the boardwalk between the steeplechase and the funhouse.

Mitzi called out from the living room. "Would you like a glass of milk or something before you go to sleep?"

"No, thanks," I said, sinking into sleep. "But I would like a glass of champagne—like at Mother's wedding."

" 'Fraid not, young man. Oh, I put some money on the kitchen table in case you wake up before I do and want to go somewhere. Good night."

"I want to go to Coney Island," I said, loud enough for Mitzi to hear. Then as sleep overcame me I said dreamily, "with you Aunt Mitzi—with you."

Sometimes, in Folsom, when I had a severe attack of the crazies I'd remember the last time Mitzi and I screwed. And I could still feel the anger I felt when I woke up to find her gone.

She'd left me two-hundred dollars and a note on the kitchen table. Sure, I remember the note. Mitzi was my life—all that was left of my life. She took care of all my needs. She stimulated my imagination as well as my balls. And if any of my wives or sweethearts or one-nighters still recall with joy my imaginative, creative skills in bed, they should send a note of thanks to Mitzi. We rehearsed for two years. And who knows. Maybe there is a planet Lam.

But, that day, when I saw the note that finished us off, I declared war on Lam. The note said: "Forgive me. I gave what I could. Zayda always spoke of karma. Maybe that was it. I am going to be married. Please go back to your mother. Love, Mitzi. P.S. Your Aunt Lillian would like to see you. Her new phone number is LUdlow 4-5780.

My first impulse on reading the note was to tear it up and leave the money on the table. But, I remembered my hungry days on the road before I reached Jackson, Mississippi, and decided to keep it and pay it back later.

So, I picked the money up and was ready to put it in my billfold. That's the way Zayda taught me. But I had a sudden change of mind. Instead of the billfold, I folded the money and the note together and stuck it in my pocket. Father's style. Then, I got my suitcase and left. I wanted to see if I could find the freaks.

Purposely avoiding Zayda's house, I walked along Kelly Street, a block away. Nothing had changed in that year. The *yentas* were still gossiping in front of the houses and kids were going back to school after lunch break. I did see gold-star banners in a few windows. You were entitled to display a gold star if you lost a son in action. Send us your children we'll give you a gold star sewed on a beautiful white silk banner which you have the privilege to display.

Maybe I'll go overseas, get killed in action, and they'll send Mitzi a gold star, I thought. Then a half a block away I spotted Harvey going into Solomon's candy store and I ran; almost dropping my suitcase, to catch up to him. And for a moment, gold stars seemed unimportant.

Solomon's was alive with kids. They were buying candy and pencils to take to school for afternoon session and giving Solomon a bad time. And there was Harvey. He was getting a chocolate egg-cream soda. I thought I'd stand there. Wait for him to notice me. Be surprised. But my heart jumped when he just stood there drinking his soda, looking right past me. I knew he'd seen me. And when I walked up to him, he started to move away. "You shouldn't have come back, Irwin," he said.

"What do you mean? We're friends."

"Not anymore. We voted you out of the club. And, anyway, we're all busy with high school now."

"What's that got to do with being friends. We always said friends for life."

"Yeah. But you broke the rules. You went to jail."

"But that was just hitchhiking—not stealing."

"Your Aunt Mitzi said your mother says you took your father's jewelry. Anyway, our parents won't let us have anything to do with you."

Mother! The peacock! Mother! The liar! Mother! I was humiliated. Infuriated. Harvey finished his soda and left. I didn't follow him. I just stood there. Looking at the kids in the candy store, laughing, telling secrets, I wondered if they all knew I'd been in jail and were whispering—laughing about me.

After Harvey had been gone for a while, I walked outside, and looked in the display window. Not really looking. Not really seeing. I was just trying to decide what to do. And maybe I looked in the window because I didn't want anyone to recognize me. Then, it struck me that old man Solomon, who'd known my Zayda and Buba and my family from the temple and who Mitzi painted a sign for—and who witnessed my Bar Mitzvah, didn't say hello to me. Well, maybe he was too busy. Maybe if I go back inside. No, I didn't risk it.

I turned away remembering the day Solomon came to Zayda's house. He was looking for Mitzi. He said "make a sign for my window. My brother—oy, he should only *plotz*—went and opened a candy store on Prospect Avenue. We ain't partners anymore. So, Mitzila, I want you should make me a sign. It should say dat I'm the original Solomon—

son of a mystic rabbi—and that I tell fortunes, and give lucky numbers and that I make big sodas—all flavors and that I got a phone booth in back of the store—and that I ain't no longer related to my brother on Prospect Avenue. Mitzila, the sign should say my brother's a faker!"

I turned back to see if the sign Mitzi painted was still there. It wasn't. And I figured he and his brother were friends again. Maybe someday the four freaks . . . No. Fuck the freaks. Someday I'd be rich and famous. Then they'll come to me. Besides, I bet Harvey and Philip and Frankie haven't been laid yet. Like me. No. They're still kids. Fuck 'em.

Aunt Lillian received me icily. "Your mother should have shipped your father's body back here to New York," she said.

"I'm sorry." I said apologetically.

"I hear you have my brother's watch and ring. They were supposed to be mine. So if you give them to me, we can be friends."

"I don't have them. Mother gave them to her new husband."

"I don't believe you. Why would your mother lie?"

"I don't know. Honest."

"You sound almost believable. I guess I taught you drama well. Listen, Irwin, tell you what. You give me my brother's jewelry, it's really mine you know, and when I die, I'll leave it to you. Promise."

I had nothing to give to her. So, I left.

Why not go see Aunt Annie? See Zayda's house—maybe for the last time. After all, that's where I was raised. That's where my memories were closely tied.

"Sure you can stay here—for a month, anyway," Aunt Annie said. "Then, I'm closing it up. Getting married. Going to California. Is it nice there?"

"I guess. Who you marrying?"

"Oh, you don't know him. We're perfect together. You'll meet him if you stay around. Hey! Maybe he can get you a job—if that's what you want—at the dress factory where he works. I'll ask him. Okay?"

"Sure. Aunt Mitzi gave me some money. It'll last a while. But I'm not going back to school. So I better get a job," I said. "Aunt Annie, was he very sick—Zayda?"

A sad shadow fell over her gay mood. "No. It was sudden. It was me—I found him. Just like he was only asleep—on the platform rocker in the garden. I was alone. Everyone else had gone out. So, I had to run to the neighbors for help. Get the doctor."

"Poor Zayda. Are you sure he had no pain?"

"Doctor said not. I believe him. But I'm afraid Zayda's death means more than I dare think: I've a feeling we won't be a family anymore. Especially now. That rotten brother of mine—who caused Zayda so much grief to begin with— didn't even show up for Buba's funeral—his own mother!" She cried for a short while, then stopped. Suddenly. It was as though she was determined. No more tears.

"The lawyer," Annie continued, more composed, "read Zayda's will. He left every penny to my brother—and said he knew my brother was sorry—he (Zayda) was sorry too and now my brother could take over and keep the family together—I just don't believe it. In the will Zayda said something about not wanting to be a donkey. Anyway. You'd think he'd have left each of us something. He couldn't have been in his right mind. So. I don't know about my sisters, but I'm contesting the will. My brother said he's selling the house. But we haven't heard from him. Can't reach him. I'd like to burn the house down. It's good you don't know your uncle. But your Zayda was a rich man. He made a lot of money from those improvements on automatic bread slicing. And what with his investments . . . a lot of money. My brother won't share."

Aunt Annie was correct about her brother. He refused to share the wealth Zayda entrusted to him. Instead he took bitter revenge for having been rejected by Zayda and instead of embracing his sisters in joyful reunion, he remained a stranger. Zayda's surge of guilt and dying dreams of hugs and kisses and happy sounds and family solidarity became dust drifting away from his grave. And I, like my Uncle Harry, became a stranger—even to myself. I sleepwalked through the undulating shadows of Zayda's dying dreams and not even a raindrop or a howling wind could wake me.

I went through the motions of life. I went to work in the dress factory. And when Zayda's house was closed down I got a furnished room in Manhattan, not far from the garment district. Work and eat and sleep. That's all I did. In a few months, I'd saved some money and decided to go back to California.

New York no longer held promise for me. Zayda's death depressed me constantly. Harvey's rejection of our friendship . . . Mitzi's coming marriage . . . the house I was raised in sold. With the exception of a movie once in a while I spent my time brooding. Even Aunt Annie had gone. I was completely alone. Mitzi . . . if she would only reconsider and resume our relationship—I thought perhaps our separation would cause her to miss me as painfully as I missed her. I yearned to see her. Talk to her. I had to gaze upon her lovely face once more.

I called Mitzi and told her I was going back to California and begged her to see me before I left. She said I couldn't come to the apartment but would meet me at Schrafft's on Broadway. "Maybe we'll even go to a movie for old time's sake."

Standing in front of the mirror, adjusting my tie, appraising myself, I wondered if Mitzi had gotten married. I was afraid to ask her on the phone. I wondered if she'd heard from mother. I hadn't written to anyone. I remember being excited over the prospect of seeing Mitzi again. I really didn't give a damn about what she had told me about morals, what we were doing was wrong, and that blood relatives "don't have sex together."

I never thought of Mitzi as a blood relative. Not like a mother. Shit. I knew that was something people didn't do with their kids. Mitzi explained that the first time we screwed. But, I just felt the rest was bullshit. Her way of dumping me for an older man.

Well, now that I had real job, even some sporty clothes just like my father, and some money saved . . . maybe . . . if she hadn't married . . . we could pick up where we left off. After all, I was going to be seventeen years old in September. Old enough to go in the Navy—with parents' permission—so I figured I was old enough to do anything else. Hell. I even had a mustache. Just like Paul Muni. And I remember, looking at myself in the mirror, smoothing my mustache hoping Aunt Mitzi would "oh" and "ah" over the way I looked, I pretended I was Muni playing the role of Zola. Hunching slightly. Stroking my chin and imagining I was addressing the jury I said:

"Ladies and gentlemen of the jury. I stand before you a condemned man. No longer anyone's son. I am now even less than a nephew. A nephew no one wants. I stand accused of stealing my father's ruby ring and gold watch. But I tell you, you will find them on my mother's husband. He is the guilty one. I stand accused of having sinned with my Aunt Mitzi. And of this I am guilty. So do with me what you will. But, I beg you, leave Mitzi be."

At Schrafft's, looking across the table, over cups of hot chocolate, at Mitzi, gazing at her wondrous face—the face that seemed to always hold the promise of magic for me—I was happy, so entranced, that I didn't pay notice to the people around us. And she did "oh" and "ah" over my Paul Muni mustache. "So, Paul Muni Altman, what are your plans now?"

"Go back to California. See if mother will sign papers for me to join the Navy—unless . . ."

"Unless what?" she interrupted.

I held my breath for moment. Then let months of frustration out. "Unless you're not married and I can stay with you. I don't care if it's wrong. I want to be with you. What did I do to make you not like me anymore?"

We sat for a moment in frozen silence. I kept my eyes on her face for any indication of what she was thinking. Then, she lifted her cup of hot chocolate and drew it to her lips. "The hot chocolate's cold," she said, putting her cup down. "Irwin, first of all, I don't only like you, I love you. And I love being with you. But, it's sick. And it's even sicker if you believe that it's okay even after I've explained how wrong it is. That means I've led your mind in a wrong direction."

Mitzi talked on. But no matter how she tried, she couldn't convince me that she wasn't rejecting me solely for an older man. "Are you married yet?" I asked, sarcastically.

"No. We've put it off a few months. He wants to save a little more money."

"Is he very old?"

"Two years older than me. And that's another thing. Say that it was okay for you and me. Say we went someplace where no one knew us. Don't you think people would wonder about us. You're so much younger than I am. And when we're older, I'll look like a tired old shoe to you. See. Anyway you look at it, it's no good . . ."

She must have seen her argument was falling on deaf ears and decided to force me to listen. "Remember, your father told you I was a 'tramp'?"

"I don't want to hear it."

"But you will listen. I am a tramp. And the reason he knew is because he did it to me—just like you do it to me. I was fifteen years old. He thought I was a virgin and really got angry when he found out I wasn't."

"I don't believe you!"

"It's true. And he told your mother. Your mother didn't believe him either—at first. And I'll tell you something else. Did you ever hear the boys in school talk about girls that'll do it for all the boys? Well, nephew, I was one of those girls. And I really took a chance—because it wasn't until I got married that I found out I couldn't have children. I could've gotten pregnant anytime . . . would you like to know who the first one was?"

"No!" I snapped. I was stunned. In a state of shock. Still, I remember clearly feeling compassion for Mitzi and the beginnings of my own guilt. And, I remember telling myself that she was lying. Just wanted to get rid of me. After all, Zayda had said women were "royalty." Could do no wrong. "Always respect . . . ." I remember confusion. Mitzi and I walked out of Schrafft's together. Said our goodbyes. And I was not to see her again. Miss her. Yes. Love her. Yes. But, see her? Only in the many women that would be drawn into my life's experience . . . only through the misty windows of my dreams would I ever see the magic in her green eyes and follow her gentle laughter through childhood's fragile shadows.

IV

Sylvia died. She was twenty-five. I was twenty-two. Our marvelous and compatible marriage of four years ended. I watched her waste away: her beautiful olive-skinned face half-burned from the X-ray treatments. Cancer of the mastoid. It took six months from the night she woke me, and asked me to call our doctor. "Most awful earache I've ever had," she cried.

I don't know how our marriage was for her. She'd always said she was happy. And because of my own pure happiness, first time since early childhood, I have no reason to believe otherwise.

Because of Sylvia, my unpleasant childhood and my equally unpleasant short hitch in the Navy had become a "Well, that's the way it was, but I'm happy now" attitude.

Mother had given permission "gladly" for me to enlist in the Navy, a nine-month career which ended with an honorable medical discharge for a severe nervous breakdown: Some asshole pushed me before I was ready to jump from a twenty-foot tower into a survival training pool while I was adjusting my life preserver. I went flying. The padding of my life jacket saved me from broken ribs. I fell against the cement runner around the pool before I went toppling in. What that asshole did to me swabbies gleefully called "grabass." So while I was not physically cracked, I did have a nervous breakdown. And I was discharged with a small, but handy, pension, and about four hundred dollars in mustering-out pay. The war was over anyway. So, it was no great loss.

Anyway, I went to Los Angeles. Got back my old job as a shoe salesman at Berland's for Ladies on Broadway, took a furnished room with board on Palm Grove Avenue, and became an active member in the neighborhood synagogue. And at one of the synagogue bazaars, I met Sylvia. I'd put my drama training, and vague memories of Buba's fortune-telling to good use at the bazaar. I wrapped a scarf—turban fashion—around my head, and transformed myself into "Isaac the Psychic."

Palms read for a quarter. Tarot cards—fifty cents. For seventy-five cents (it's a good cause, for the City of Hope Foundation) you could have palm and cards. I told all the young girls they would marry doctors, lawyers, rabbis, "and I see two gorgeous children—a boy and a girl."

"So, who needs a doctor, or lawyer or a rabbi?" Sylvia said, shoving the cards toward me, "I'd be happy to have a date with Isaac the Psychic for a movie."

"A girl with such gorgeous brown eyes, deserves only the best—at least someone who owns a good kosher delicatessen—at least that. I have nothing. Not a cent."

"Good. Then I'll take you to the movies. My treat . . . or if you have a couple of dollars we'll go dutch."

She was lovely. So open. So pretty. I did want to go on a date with her. But I'd been shy of girls. The only "girl" I'd ever been close to was Aunt Mitzi and that . . . well, it didn't count. Besides there were still strings of guilt tied to Mitzi. Only a date. A movie. Harmless. Besides, the few girls I'd dated had been "Mama's beautiful daughter," and believed a vagina (which I was never allowed to get acquainted with) was worth the combined incomes of ten doctors or at least one Beverly Hills gynecologist. The fact that their fathers might have been tailors or meat cutters or fancy steam pressers who stood on their feet fourteen hours a day to keep them in expensive frocks didn't matter to them. They were raised to believe they deserved better than a menial laborer. And let it be known that they were looking for husbands who at least had a rich father.

Maybe Sylvia was the first of the new age of female awareness. Whatever it was she had, I knew I'd enjoy spending some hours with her. "Look. I'm not exactly broke. I do have a job. So, I can take you to the movies. And I'd like to."

"Tonight? If it's not tonight, forget it." Taken by surprise—happy surprise—I said, "Tonight. What time and where shall I pick you up?"

"Let's see. It's two o'clock now. How about five? I live on Palm Grove, twenty-nine-forty-four. We eat at five-thirty. Don't be late."

"Eat?" another surprise.

"My mother and father wouldn't have it any other way. Neither would I. After all, how can I marry someone unless I know about their table manners? Write it down. Twenty-nine-forty-four Palm Grove. What's your name?"

"Irwin," I replied. "I'll remember." I laughed. "I live a block away at twenty-eight-thirty-six."

"I have only one question . . . ," she said as she started to leave the booth. For a moment I panicked. I thought she was going to ask me how old I was. And I perceived I was a bit younger than she. But my fears disappeared when she smiled, "Are you planning on becoming a rabbi?"

"Oh, a long time ago, when my Zayda was alive I thought of it—but not anymore."

"Are you sure?"

"Yes, I'm certain. Why?"

"Why? Well, what kind of job is a rabbi for a Jewish boy." She laughed. Then left. My solar plexus did a gypsy dance.

I guess she liked my table manners. Her wonderful parents approved, for sure. And the fact that Sylvia was twenty-one, three years older than myself, didn't matter. Which was in itself unusual. Because in the nineteen-forties, chronological age weighed heavily in the mating balance. Anyway, a year after we met, we were married. And not only did I have a loving wife, I had a family again. Sylvia's parents treated me like I was their own son.

During our one year engagement I had because of Sylvia's suggestion, gone to school on the G.I. Bill, and learned a trade. I'd become a hairdresser. Sylvia had been a hairdresser since age sixteen. If father were alive he'd have hemorrhaged. But when Sylvia and I began speaking seriously of marriage she said: "Selling shoes is okay. But, learn a trade. At least look it over. Today, if you're a man and dress hair—

even if you're just mediocre—the women will come to you if you worked out of a garage. But you'll be a good stylist. I can help you. If you don't like it you can always go back to selling shoes and looking at legs. And when you graduate Beauty School, I'll give you a present. Maybe you'll like it better than your diploma." So, in nineteen-forty-seven, Irwin Altman and Sylvia Kavetsky were married. And there I was a nineteen- year-old bridegroom with a twenty-two-year-old beauty of a wife and a new mama and papa—Joy! Did Sylvia give me my graduation present? Yes. But not until our wedding night. Well, in the forties a girl still had to have a government-inspected stamp to prove her virginity.

We both worked damned hard. We scrimped and saved from our paychecks. I styled hair in the May Company Department Store beauty salon for fifty dollars plus commission a week. And because of my experience in selling I earned about ten dollars in commissions every week. With tips, I managed to swing seventy-five dollars—sometimes. And I enjoyed my work. Hell, I was used to being around women.

Sylvia worked in Beverly Hills. She had a movie-star clientele. So she made more money than I did. "So what," she'd say, "it's all in the same pocketbook." That was true. She managed the money. Skillfully.

And, by nineteen-forty-eight, we swung a deal and bought our own salon on Beverly Boulevard near Fairfax—Kosher Valley. We paid nine hundred dollars for it. A hole in the wall. Run-down. We scrubbed, painted, shined, laughed, argued, and finally put up our grand-opening banner: "Stylists to the Stars"—Opening Special: Haircut, Shampoo, Style—Ninety-nine cents!

The ladies lined up. Sylvia and I worked side by side. Our own clientele had followed us to our salon. And because of the opening special we added new customers. Worked our asses off. And it was good. Brought corned beef or pastrami sandwiches and delicious kosher pickles from Canter's on Fairfax and ate in the supply room—standing up. And it was good. And Sylvia got pregnant. And it was pure joy. She worked along with me until a week before our daughter Rachelle was born. And that was happiness. The same time space next door to our salon became vacant. We rented it. Broke through the walls, bought more equipment. Hired people. At the same time, the CBS Studios opened across the street. And some of the women who worked at CBS joined our clientele. And it was good. And it was hard work. And it was fun. And Sylvia and I were happy.

Everything we had was paid for. Even our daughter. Sylvia stayed home with Rachelle. But she did come by the salon every day with our daughter. "Just to see how you are and pick up the money," she'd laugh.

Sundays we'd drive to the beach. Our new family. Fridays it was dinner at Sylvia's folks. My mother? She came around. But it always upset me. And the Kavetskys couldn't figure it out. "How can a mother and a child not get along." I never told them why. And they didn't pry. Sylvia knew. But she didn't tell.

Nineteen-fifty-one: Sylvia died. And for the second time, since the day my mother dubbed me her nephew—I died again.

Everything was gone. Sylvia gone. The salon sold to cover medical bills. And my daughter and I moved in with Sylvia's folks. It was mourning and tears every day. And I took an overdose of sleeping pills. It didn't work. I cut my wrists and took an overdose of sleeping pills to go with it. It didn't work. But I did get committed to the Veterans Hospital in Brentwood.

While in the hospital the Kavetskys had gone to court and somehow managed to get "temporary" custody of my three-year-old daughter. Well, I was nuts. That's how come. No, I never injured anyone. Just myself.

Upon being released from the hospital with less than a hundred dollars to my name, I bought an expensive doll for Rachelle, and went to see her.

"It's not good you should be around your daughter now.

Maybe later . . . maybe. But not now," Sylvia's parents told me. So, I took my clothes, threw them in the back seat of my car and drove to San Diego. I don't remember feeling anything except determination to get my daughter back.

San Diego. A job dressing hair at Walker's Department Store. I sent money orders to the Kavetskys every week for Rachelle. But they still wouldn't let me see her. I decided to see a lawyer, and took one afternoon from work. My appointment was in the late afternoon so I decided to have lunch at a busy sandwich shop across the street from Walker's.

It was a typical lunch hour. The restaurant was busy and crowded; people gulping sandwiches and beverages glancing feverishly at their watches and demanding executive service for a dollar plus a quarter tip. Strangers shared tables. Women eyeing cute guys. Men making with mating calls, "Mind if I share your table," they'd quack. But all the while sizing the chick up and down. It'd be more direct to say, "Wanna play house for an hour—forty minutes, actually. Gotta be back at work by one-o-five, latest." I've often amused my brain with pictures of people in the luncheonette dropping their ham-on-ryes and breaking out into one big orgy. Now, that would be one hell of a lunch break. More honest than a soggy ham-on-rye.

So, I was looking for a place to sit. The only seat open was with an impeccably dressed businessman-type in his thirties who was scribbling figures on a napkin. "Mind if I sit here," I smiled.

"No, not at all," he said.

"Figuring the budget?" I asked, referring to the scribbled figures on the napkin, recalling how Sylvia and I would sit at Canter's on Fairfax, after we closed the salon for the day, and do exactly that. Sylvia. My mind drifted momentarily and my smile faded into a moment of gloom.

"No. Not the budget," he said. "Just working up figures for a prospectus. Name's Jim—Jim LaFamento." He seemed friendly. The kind of person people take to on the spot. And I felt in the mood for a friend.

"Irwin Altman," I said. "LaFamento? There was a girl in my music class in grade school. Margie LaFamento. Had a beautiful voice."

"No relation I'm afraid. But, tell you what, Irwin, if that waitress doesn't get here soon, I'll sing like hell for you," he laughed. And it struck me that he would be capable of doing just that; he had a charm and wit about him; no one could possibly become annoyed at his mischievousness. He was the kind of guy that could say "fuck you all" to a church group and make it sound like the Sermon on the Mount. "Good location, this joint," he continued, "our bank holds the paper on it."

I was impressed. He'd told me what he did to make it in the world. And didn't ask me what I did. Proper. Zayda always said, "Don't pry. If someone wants you should know something they'll tell you." Zayda would've liked Jim.

Deciding Jim was okay, I said, "I dress hair at Walker's—across the street. Haven't been there long. Just about two months. Came down from Los Angeles."

"Los Angeles, huh. I got an ex-wife there . . ."

The waitress came and took our orders and hurried away. While we waited for her hopefully quick return, Jim proceeded to tell me that when he got out of the Army, he thought he'd surprise his wife and not tell her he was on the way home. " . . . overseas I'd heard a lot of talk about women screwing around on the home front—but I didn't figure it would happen to me . . . I've been married and divorced again, since. You married?"

"No. Widowed. My wife passed away a few months ago," I said. And by the time I'd finished telling Jim a few details, we'd finished our lunch. And were sipping on our coffees.

"Tough break," he said, genuinely. "Say. Tell you what, Irwin, sounds like your wife's illness wiped you out money-wise, as well as the pain of your having lost a loved one. Why don't you come on over to the bank. Right now. Put in a loan application. I'll take care of it personally. Hell," he laughed, "we can split the money and go to Mexico."

"Sounds tempting," I said, thinking I was stroking back what sounded like a little harmless joke. "But," I continued, seriously, "I don't have any collateral. I really am wiped out. And I don't make enough at Walker's Beauty Salon to do all the things I have to do, like live; and, send money for my daughter."

He seemed not to pay attention to what I was saying. "How about twenty thousand dollars? Would that help?"

Feeling the conversation was leading to no plausible end, I said, "Look, Jim. It's getting late, and I have an appointment." I got up to leave.

"Before you go. Let me ask you a question. Where are your priorities? I just offered you twenty thousand dollars. Took a chance doing it. You could tell someone. But I sense that you're not the kind to rubbermouth. And if I'm wrong about you—you couldn't prove a one-to-one conversation like this. So, what say? Want to try your hand?"

I was stunned. I sat back down. He was serious. Damned serious. And at that moment, everything else seemed so futile, anyway, so I asked, "But why me? Why a stranger?"

"Stranger? Well, for practical reasons, to begin with. Every one of my friends would think I was nuts if they knew I wanted to rob a bank. My bank at that. And maybe I am nuts. And I don't have an associate at the bank I'd care to discuss this matter with. So, why not you—a stranger. Besides. People are never strangers. Not unless you want to go through life alone. So," he said, sticking his hand out to me, "say hello to a stranger."

According to Jim's instructions, I quit my job at Walker's. Then, details needed to be worked out. Jim, being a loan officer at the bank was one small hurdle crossed. But only a small jump. Compared to what was to come. A loan the size he spoke of would take more than just his signature for approval. But he had enough "juice" to push it through to the big signatures needed—providing we could supply "on paper" the necessary collateral. "A financial statement in the form of a bank account. And an office. And a phone," Jim said, concentrating. "Let's see . . . about making you a young man who just took over the family business in Los Angeles. And now you want to expand. I'll rent an office for you. We're a small bank. Management wears lots of hats. So, I can go through the motions, the initial checkout on you. I've been with the bank since I was a kid. I was a messenger for them before I went into the service. And when I came back, they gave me a desk job. 'Nothing too good for our boys,' the old man said. They trust me. Trust any sap stupid enough to work for the kind of money they pay—greedy bastards. 'Nothing too good.' That's what I get. Nothing. Find a greedy man and I'll find you the key to the world. But you've got to convince the greedies that you're naive. And if you can convince them you're naive and have money to go with your naivete—let them believe they can slick you out of some of your money, you'll be wined and dined, have your ass kissed—on both cheeks and even get your prick mistaken for an all-day sucker . . ."

It was all Jim's talk of wine and dinners and fancy women that made his proposition more interesting to me than the money itself. He'd say "not just ordinary women. But women who've got an education. Women who smell and dress like delicate Oriental gardens, and stuff their inherent nature to nag down the toilet—if they believe you have that long green stuff. And, if daddy's left them a bundle, no matter how much, it's never enough for them—they want yours too; and are willing to go to any length to get it. Even to the extent of 'tiding you over till your mythical inheritance' or whatever you've contrived comes due."

"And even if they don't have money it's still fun. Lots of lonely nights can be filled with big tits."

I remember hoping that not all "fancy women" had "big tits," because I'd already developed a taste for tiny titties. Like Aunt Mitzi. "Do all your lady friends have big tits," I asked Jim.

"Every one. You bet," he bragged, shaping the air into female figures.

Well, I figured there had to be a few not-so-fancy women somewhere in that world in the air Jim shaped in front of me. Maybe even some women who'd appreciate a man who worked out of town a lot but always brought home the money. Maybe even someone who really needed me and I could tell her, "Well, the money goes with the package." Maybe she'd be having a hard time of it and I could help.

Maybe, I could send Aunt Mitzi some money. Her husband, I'd heard, was not doing so well. That would make her sorry she didn't stay with me. And, for certain with the amount of money Jim talked about, I could give my daughter everything in the world. But for one-hundred-percent-certain, I'd leave all the mammoth tits in the world for the Jims of the world.

It took two months for Jim's plan to come to a head. And he'd invested some money in it. "Gotta spend it to make it," he'd say.

He proceeded by showing me how to change my name.

"Easy," he coached. "Just go to Chicago, or New York; don't want to get birth certificates that are local. Might have family around. Anyway, go to the hall of records and research the death certificates. Find kids who've died about the time you were born. Don't get all the same county. Just bring back the information from the death certificates—all of it."

After we had that information Jim sent for certified copies of the birth certificates belonging to the kids who passed away.

"Now, take this stuff," he said referring to the certificates, "and get four driver's licenses—four different names. You'll have a bit of traveling around to do."

I got the driver's licenses and Jim said, "Here's two hundred dollars. Take it and open four checking accounts. Fifty dollars each." He gave me a list of four banks geographically separated so as to allow a minimum of eight days to clear checks from one bank to the other.

In the early nineteen-fifties it took checks anywhere from a week to two weeks to clear, providing the banks were small and if they were far enough apart, like from San Francisco to San Diego.

I followed Jim's instructions, exactly. And the stage was set. Timing was critical. "Now, Irwin," Jim was beginning to show signs of controlled edginess, "we are ready for the winner's circle. First you write a check for seventy-thousand dollars on the bank in San Francisco and deposit it in the bank in Los Angeles. Then write a seventy-thousand-dollar check on the bank in Los Angeles and deposit it in my bank in San Diego. Then, you write a check from my bank for the same amount and deposit it in the bank in Chula Vista. Then, write a seventy-thousand dollar check on the bank in Chula Vista and deposit it in the bank you started with in San Francisco. Then, my good man, the circle is complete. By the time you've done a bit of traveling from bank to bank, the checks will have cancelled each other out. And as long as you don't try to withdraw money on those accounts you're okay. Not only okay but you have, on paper, two-hundred-and-eighty-thousand dollars. The next step is the sticky one."

Jim's plan was to have me apply at his bank for a fifty-thousand dollar loan using the seventy-thousand dollar bogus account as collateral. He'd "stay on top of the whole thing." Then he'd take the thirty-thousand dollars, which went a long way in the early nineteen-fifties, and go to a favorite spot of his in Mexico, open a "high-class whorehouse. Catering only to Mexican businessmen and government officials. Got my eye on a beautiful house. Swimming pool and everything for five thousand. Things are cheap in Mexico," he said greedily. "I've got this woman down there—gorgeous *senorita*—I'll marry her, and that way I can stay there. You can be sure of one thing, Irwin. Even when my bank wises up the people I know in Mexico—all those high government officials, all crooks themselves—won't let me be extradited back to the U.S. Especially since I'll give the right ones a slice of the action."

My own plans were not nearly as exciting as Jim's. No *senoritas*—at least not in Mexico. Oh, I might take a trip down there—see what it's like, I thought, but that was all. And I had no intentions of opening whorehouses or getting involved with sleazy officials here or there.

I, in fact, wondered what Jim would do on only thirty-thousand dollars. But it was a good lump sum. Fluid cash. Cash you could use right now, and he didn't have to save years to put it together. Well, maybe he figured the whorehouse would take care of the rest.

Me? Well, I knew there were consequences if I got caught.

Jim laid it out: "Worse that'll happen, especially since you don't have a police record, you'll get a year in the pokey."

Well, I hadn't been in jail since the day I got picked up for hitchhiking in Mississippi when I was fifteen. And, though it was an unpleasant memory, it didn't seem close enough to keep me from jumping into Jim's bag with him. Twenty-thousand dollars. I could do a lot with that kind of money. Especially for my little girl. She took top priority. Anything else was secondary. Especially a whorehouse.

The events that followed caused me to decide never to crime with a partner again. Never discuss my crime plans with anyone. And not crime unless absolutely necessary. The night before we were to bring our plans to a climax, I paced my room feverishly. I had no appetite. And I did one hell of a lot of second thinking. I even thumbed through a Bible I'd bought one particularly depressive night.

And while I read from the "Book of Begats"—Genesis— deciding that the original populace of our planet did what Mitzi and I did, the phone rang. It was Jim in a panic. " . . . Change of plans. Nothing to worry about. Meet me at the Jack-in-the-Box on El Cajon Boulevard in a half hour."

Over a late coffee, Jim said, "The old man had a heart at- tack. He's laid up in the hospital. Need his signature for a loan that size. Don't want to ask our Vice-President. He's just a naturally suspicious person. So, this is what we'll do. . . ."

The following morning, I walked into the bank, and headed for the row of tellers' cages. There were a few customers on line at every cage and a bank guard wandering around. So, I chose a line and waited my turn. I kept looking from the corner of my eye for Jim but didn't see him anywhere. I thought I'd have diarrhea.

There was a secretary-type chick just ahead of me doing a transaction for her employer. I was next and still no sight of Jim. And by then I thought I'd buckle under from the pressure of controlling my nerves.

"Can I help you please," said the teller. I was so engrossed and nervous that I hadn't noticed the secretary-type leave.

And I hadn't moved up to the teller's cage yet. So, I walked up to the teller, and following Jim's instructions, in a business-like tone, I said, "Yes, thank you. I have a transaction to do in cash . . ." I removed my checkbook from my inside pocket and felt as though the eyes of the bank guard were staring at me. But I kept cool. Didn't turn around. " . . . A large sum. I'll need one of your bank sacks." Then without another word, I tore a check from the book, picked up the customer convenience pen in front of me, wrote a check for fifty-thousand dollars, slipped it through the cage, and held my breath.

The teller didn't show any signs of emotion. It was just as Jim described the night before. The transaction was not unusual. Then, just as Jim also described at the Jack-in-the-Box, the teller said, "I'll have to get one of the bank officers to okay this." And just as she put the "closed" board across the slot in her cage, a door, just off the side, opened and out walked Jim carrying a small stack of memos. I felt relieved and smiled. But, he pretended not to notice me, and walked right past the teller.

"Oh, Mr. LaFamento," the teller said to Jim. "This gentleman would like to have this in cash. Would you okay it." Then, she took the "closed" sign down.

Feigning a quizzical look, Jim said, "I know I've seen you in here before—several times—but I'll still need some identification. Especially with your signature. And may I see your checkbook please."

I handed over my identification and checkbook. Jim turned away leaving the teller to keep me company. And after what seemed forever he returned. "Sorry to keep you waiting. Everything's in order. How would you like the money?"

"In hundred-dollar bills. In the bands," I said, "And can you spare one of your bank sacks and a guard for about ten minutes. My office is just down the street."

"Generally, we have two guards on duty. But not today. And I can't take our one guard away from the floor. Anything could go wrong. Any given moment. Might have a holdup. Lots of crooks around, you know. Tell you what. I have an attache case. We could put the money in there— better than a bank sack. And I could get you a taxi.''

"No. No taxis, thanks. The attache case will do. I'll return it later."

"Fine," Jim said. "I'll bring it to you in a few moments."

Walking that block to the office Jim had rented for me, with a case full of money, more money than I'd ever seen or held, was somehow comforting. I began to regain my composure and realized, thanks to Jim LaFamento, I now had a unique avocation.

And that evening, in the office, when Jim handed me twenty-thousand dollars out of the attache case, I was overcome by a feeling of power and excitement I'd never had before.

Jim and I parted company that same evening. And each of us went in our own direction. "Remember," were Jim's parting words, "if you ever decide to visit Mexico—you know how to find me. You're a good partner. You're conscientious. Work hard. I trust you."

Since then, I've been to Mexico often. But, never looked Jim up. Never had a strong desire to see him.

"This is to take care of Rachelle," I said to Mrs. Kavetsky as I handed her a cashier's check for twenty-thousand dollars. "I won it in a big poker game."

"You're making a wise decision, Irwin. A man by himself can't take care of such a little child. We'll give her the best. Are you going to stay in Los Angeles?"

I knew I had to keep moving. But I didn't want to talk about it. And unhappily, I knew when I took Rachelle in my arms, it would be a terribly long time, if ever, before I'd see her again. And though I was overcome with guilt regarding Rachelle, and the reason I couldn't be anywhere close to her, my decision had been made. And I was the one who made it. I was going to do another caper. And another. And another. I was going to burn up the world.

"I don't know if I'll stay in L.A. or not. I'll keep in touch. Just remember. Don't tell anyone I gave you this money. Not anyone."

"Irwin. I won't ask you where . . . I don't want to know. But somehow I know."

VI

Having handed all the money I'd taken from the swindle in San Diego to Mrs. Kavetsky for the care of Rachelle, I left Los Angeles. My entire bankroll now consisted of a hundred-fifty dollars. Money I'd managed to save from the expense money Jim LaFamento invested in me. Jim's total investment for the fifty-thousand was just under two-thousand dollars. Fifty-thousand dollars is not a bad return for two-thousand dollars and two months' effort. Providing you're willing to risk going to prison for it.

For most people into crime there is no such thing as a one and only. For me it gained momentum. And my life became lonely. I was willing to risk going to prison. But I was not willing to be lonely. I seemed always to be searching for a woman to love. To care for. Someone to give a damn about. And someone who would give a damn about what happened to me.

But by the time my first wife passed away there had already been the loss of three women in my life. Two who rejected me. And one by death. And I believed that such gloomy conditions were my Karma—a punishment, a "lesson for the growth of the soul . . ." as Zayda had spoken about so often years before.

Well, maybe, I told myself, I'd done something horrendous to a woman in a past life. So, in this life, I would compensate by lavishing women, who were drawn into my present life experience, with the highest possible good—emotionally and financially. Especially financially. And by so doing I would free my Karma. Right now. I would complete my assignment in hell. And I would do so in this lifetime. Also, I managed to develop the idea that the poor soul I'd done so much damage to in a life past was reincarnated, and, if I could find her, no matter where she was—even if she happened to be married—I could hand her the world. Even if I had to steal it. And she, in turn, would forgive me for having hurt her in the life before. Then, together we would raise my daughter. Pretty damned romantic: the man who stole the world and laid it at the feet of his lady. But the search for her was futile. And by the time I went to prison, I'd gathered one lady after the other. Too many ladies. More than one person could handle in one lifetime and still maintain sanity.

Furthermore I even entertained the notion that Aunt Mitzi was a strong candidate for my reincarnated lady. The love I believed destroyed.

Armed with these weighty ideas, I left Los Angeles. And laid a thousand dollars worth of hot checks on the road to San Francisco. Why San Francisco? It was as a good a city as any to begin the search for my Cinderella.

San Francisco. With the money from the bogus checks I passed, I rented a one-booth beauty shop on Sutter Street. And took an apartment nearby. Ad in the paper: Mr. Irwin of Hollywood—"Hair Stylist to the Stars." And I began to attract a clientele. Being a hairstylist eliminated the necessity for me to comb through the cocktail lounges of San Francisco in search of my lady. The ladies came to me. And because I was a good stylist they returned for more. And among those heads of wet hair and bobby pins I fell in love, instantly, with Beth Ann. And, instantly, I shaped her coal black hair into wispy bangs that fell over her soft, fire-green eyes. And, instantly, I bought her a wardrobe that flattered the slim lines of her body. And instantly I bought her a diamond ring which I slipped on her finger one night over cocktails and candlelight. And, instantly, I told her, "From now on, your worries are over, Beth Ann. You can give up that secretarial job and I'll take care of you. Even any bills you may have right now. I'll pay them."

"But I don't want to get married just yet, you understand," she cooed. "I'd like for us to try it first. I don't want to get married until I'm completely out of debt. It's so wonderful to know a man like you. I believe I could even learn to love you. What a beautiful ring. It must have cost you a fortune."

"Don't give it another thought. Money's no object," I said. And that was true. Money was never an object. Not as long as

I could lay my hands on a checkbook. I'd just pat my breast pocket, and boast that I had plenty of money. Didn't have to work if I didn't want to. "But my work—is important to me."

I did enjoy hair styling. Being around the ladies. I had my pick of women. And, no, I was not always one hundred percent professional. When the ladies teased and joked—I teased and joked. And, there were moments when a lovely lady would rub a gentle elbow into my groin while I moved around the styling chair combing her hair. When that happened—after being certain it wasn't a slip of the elbow—I'd return her favor with a soft brush of her breasts as I untied her comb-out cape.

That's the way Beth Ann and I became involved. "Oh," she smiled. "I see that hair is not the only thing you know how to handle to perfection. Why don't you come over to my place for dinner some night."

After that, I fixed her hair "on the house." A guy, styling hair, could soon go broke using my method of seduction. But I had another source of income: a book of blank checks from which I would draw whatever amount of cash I desired.

Discovering that we were both interested in the occult, Beth Ann and I struck it off without a hitch. Oh, there was more than just our mutual interest in occult sciences. She had one hell of a lot of bills and a marvelous body. And I was willing to take an interest in both. Life for me was just as Jim LaFamento had told me it would be: "Create the illusion of having money and even the Queen will spread her legs . . . I suppose if the money's only an illusion it's sort of like rape by conversion—ah, what the hell. It's all in fun."

Well, maybe it was "fun" for Jim. But not for me. I've rarely been with a woman I didn't have loving feelings for. And when it came time to separate from them it hurt me. Deeply. And I'd think about Jim LaFamento laughing his way through the big tits of the world. Apparently that's all women meant to him. But the women in my life—even though briefly—were my total life.

And some magic must have occurred in the evenings spent with them discussing Kant and Hesse and dissecting Aleister Crowley—the living demon. And, some magic must have occurred when we experimented with E.S.P., fortune-telling and past-life recall. For whatever the reason, there has never been a woman in my life who did not share these interests with me from the moment of our meeting. Even Beth Ann. The first time we met and I styled her hair she said, "How about if I read your palm instead of leaving you a tip?"

She did read my palm. And she did forecast: "Serious problem—soon. But don't go by what I say. I'm just learning to read palms." The woman had a great future.

One day, as I was closing my salon, a woman I hadn't seen before greeted me at the door. "Are you Irwin?" she asked. It was a familiar question. All the new people coming into my shop asked my name.

"Yes, I am," I said. "Did you want an appointment for a hairstyle?"

"No," she smiled. "I am a policewoman—there are two policemen standing outside—so, no funny stuff, because I can take you myself. You're under arrest! Just keep moving out the door." I did just that. And it wasn't until I was completely out the doorway that I saw the two giants. Well, compared to my short frame those cops were giants. Even the lady cop. She was big. One of the men slapped handcuffs on my wrists. It hurt. Handcuffs always hurt. Then, the three of them escorted me to a police car which was parked about halfway down the street. Embarrassing as hell. Arrested by a woman. And I was equally mortified by the people on the street who watched as the three giants prodded me into the rear of the police car.

The lady cop said, "Well, little man, looks like you've been busy." Then, they all three had a good laugh. Finding me was no problem. My fingerprints were all over my bogus checks. And I had been printed when I joined the Navy. So their search for me was made easy. Not only did they know who they wanted, but the trail of checks I'd laid from Los

Angeles to San Francisco led directly to me. "You must have wanted to get caught," said the lady cop. "Anyone that uses their own name wants to get caught. Right, fellas?" She said to her male counterparts.

After booking me and packing me in the slammer, the cops questioned me: "Where's LaFamento?"
   "Who?"
   "C'mon wise guy—LaFamento, your crime partner. Better tell us. We've got enough on you to salt you away for a long time." They sounded convincing. And in the early fifties cops used rubber hoses, fists, and billy clubs on "uncooperative" subjects. They didn't fail to let me know it either. " . . . how about a blanket party. You were in the service. You ever had a blanket party?"
   Blanket parties: Wrap one naked human being up in a blanket. Then let loose a half-a-dozen sadist cops wearing thick-soled leather shoes or pointed boots. Stand by and watch the action as they grunt, and stomp the shit out of the man, or woman, the helpless soul wrapped in the blanket. Then, listen to them laugh as they carry the half-dead carcass off and throw it into a cell.
   There's more than one person pushing themselves around in wheelchairs today because of a snapped spine inflicted by the boys in blue. Time was, a wino could get picked up by the cops, have his skull kicked in, then be dragged into a court-room by his heels, in chains, and hear himself accused of as-saulting an officer and resisting arrest. And the only wit-nesses were the cops who beat him. They'd stand in front of the judge feigning embarrassed wide-eyed innocence. Ad-dressing the court in flat emotionless tones: "He's a danger-ous one, your honor. Picked him up on skid row. Had an empty wine bottle concealed in his coat pocket. First, we were just going to see if we could get him over to the jail to sleep it off. But then he reaches for his bottle—real mean-like. Well, he swings—naturally we had to subdue him. Danger-ous man!"

Anyway, I wasn't taking a chance on a beating. So, I decided to lie: "LaFamento double-crossed me. Took all the money and disappeared—dirty son-of-a-bitch. And the last I could figure, he's in Chicago somewhere."

"C'mon. We know you gave that money to that Beth Ann broad to stash for you. Don't fuck with us, cocksucker."

The assholes were trying to bait me. But they chose the wrong worm. At least, now I knew they didn't know what I did with the money. And I wasn't offering. So, I said, "Beth Ann knows nothing about me. I told you what happened. There's nothing more to tell you. Nothing."

"You mean your riding the beef all on your own? What's LaFamento going to do—pay you off when you get out of prison?"

I didn't answer, but I remember thinking it would be a nice gesture on LaFamento's part if there were some money for my not giving him away. And for whatever reason they must have had, they decided against questioning me further.

So, after laying around the San Francisco jail four months I was finally taken to court. Four months without seeing a lawyer! (Though one was appointed to me.) Four months without any contact with the world outside. Four months to count cockroaches and eat a slimy soup we prisoners called "Green Death." Four months without a bath. Four months lying on a dirty blanket on a steel cot—no mattress. Four months without a change of clothes. Four months without a sound other than steel slamming against steel and fists slamming against faces and ribs. Four months without a scream. No screams from the beaten. Finally after four months, facing a comfortable, well-fed judge, I recall painfully that I would have much rather have had a conversation about the whole matter, in private, than stand limp and dirty in handcuffs in a courtroom filled with spectators.

The comfortable-looking judge asked my attorney if he were ready to proceed.

"No," said the lawyer, "no, your honor we are not. I have not had an opportunity to discuss this case with my client." I wondered where the hell he'd been while I was counting cockroaches.

"How much time will you need, counselor?"

"Oh, at least another two weeks, your honor."

"Two weeks!" I panicked. My brain swam. I passed out. Luckily, it happened in a courtroom. If I'd have fainted in jail the jailers would have left me there. But, since it happened in open court in front of spectators, the judge ordered me to San Francisco General Hospital.

In the hospital the section reserved for the jail was the psychiatric ward. It was locked. Locked and barred. But there were clean sheets. And decent food. And I was out of my dirty clothes and in a clean hospital gown. And there were employees that spoke to you, wearing fresh white starched smocks. Even if it was only to say, "Next time you get out of that bed I'm gonna strap you in it." I stayed in bed as ordered. Finally, after I'd asked enough times for a bedpan someone said, "Hey, Altman, you got a weak bladder? Do you know how to get out of that bed?" And after that I was boss of the bed. And nothing more was said about my getting in or out. And I could even walk around a bit.

And as I began to recover from my collapse I visited and talked with the other patients. One cantankerously beautiful black man left me with a lasting impression. They called him Nigger-Jesus. Employees and some patients tormented him. They teased him. They deliberately set out to anger him. And they even took his Bible away. Just to watch him flare up. "Don't mess wit' me. Don't mess wit' me. Ah'll put you in hell—you keep messin' wit' me . . . gimme back my Bible you bastahds. Gimme back my Bible an ah'll climb back on da cross for alla ya muthafuckas."

Zayda once told me, "If you call someone crazy long enough, sometimes they get crazy. If someone's a sourpuss like old man Yankel, you should tell him what a nice smile he has. Tell him enough times and he'll smile at your wedding."

So, on one of my tours of the ward I decided to stop by and

say hello to the old black man. "You know," I said, "everytime I look at you I feel good. It's your smile."

"Your fulla sheeet. Ah don't smile for no one. Not in dis machine."

"C'mon," I said. "You do smile. And this is a hospital ward. Not a machine." And I wondered about him. Misery all his life. Misery from being poor. Misery and untold torment because he was black. And even in the public hospital they tormented him. Even the blacks—his own people—called him "crazy Nigger-Jesus."

"Everything's a machine, boy. Even you. You're a white-people machine."

"I'd prefer to believe I'm a human being. Just like you."

"Well, ah can see you don' wanna talk no sense, so, we ain't got nothin' t'say. G'wan back to your bed. Git outa heah. Someday you'll know. Evertings a machine. Even God . . .'specially God. 'cause 'less yo drop some change in da God machine God ain't gonna do sheeet fo' ya. An' ah never had much change to spare—so, da God machine nevah done sheeet fo' me. Tell ya anudder ting, boy," he shouted, "Even does women—deyse machines—slot machines. Try puttin' an empty hand in a woman's drawers—ya won' get a ting outa it—no matter how you jiggle 'round. But effen ya got a handful a change ta stick in dat slot, ya gonna stand knee deep in gumballs. Even Jesus—he's a machine—a washin' machine. Peoples always trowin' dem dirty drawers in da Jesus machine—effen dey got enough change to trow in wit it, dem drawers come back snow white."

After about a week when my court-appointed lawyer came to visit me, "Good news, Altman," he beamed.

"You mean they're taking me back to the jail?"

"Don't try to be funny—you can't afford the luxury right now. Anyway, how'd you like to go to a mental hospital instead of prison . . . not for long. Just for observation. About ninety days. Could be longer. The longer the better. If they keep you eight or nine months, the judge will dismiss the case. San Diego D.A. says if they keep you up here and prosecute you for the checks you bounced around this part of the country—he'll drop the charges down there. They don't see how they can get any of that money back. And when they found out that you flipped in court here they were afraid you might cop an insanity plea. Too expensive. After all. It's not as though you have a long record."

"I don't understand. You mean to say if I'm willing to go to a hospital I don't have to go to jail."

"Well, that depends on what the doctors up there say. If they decide it was the pressure of your wife's death . . ."

"They know about that?" I interrupted.

"They know everything. Know you flipped out in the Navy. Know you flipped out when your wife died. And when they spoke to your mother-in-law and she told them you never had more than a thousand dollars at one time in your life, they decided you could be telling the truth about LaFamento screwing you. So they're looking in Chicago for him—and the money. They decided if you had any money stashed away you'd have bailed yourself out of jail."

That was true. I sure as shit would have bailed out. If I could. And Mrs. Kavetsky didn't tell about the money. "Well, what do you suggest I do?" I asked the lawyer.

"I can almost assure you—that with your record—if you go to the hospital, you won't even come back to jail. That's how the legal machine works. Oh, by the way, the police gave me the keys to your car—and I moved it to my house. That okay? You can get it when you're free."

"Sure. It's okay." What else could it be but "okay."

The lawyer knew his stuff. Six months in the hospital and the case against me was dismissed. And, know what? I saw a doctor, only once. When I was admitted. All the rest of the time I enjoyed the fresh air and the girls. Especially, I enjoyed the girls. We had group therapy. And I remember someone said, "Your whole problem is your mother, Irwin." But I never spoke of Mitzi. I figured my whole problem was getting mixed up with Jim LaFamento and as long as I stayed away from people like that my problems were over.

My small Navy disability pension had caught up to me in the hospital, and by the time I'd left I had some money saved. Enough to get a furnished room in San Francisco and keep myself in meals until I could find a job. No more crime. Just work. Work. Find a nice girl. Get married. Get my daughter. For sure, I thought. Marriage would solve all my problems.

VII

Over martinis at a backstage party given by the Lamplighters, San Francisco's Gilbert and Sullivan light opera company, Theresa and I decided to get married. We had met at Macy's Department Store Beauty Salon where, after getting out of the hospital, I managed to land a job. Unlike most of the women I'd become involved with in the months I worked at Macy's, Theresa didn't make an impression on me until she came back to the salon for a second time. She was, and still is, lovely to my eyes: expressive gray eyes, blonde hair and a neat full figure. It was the first time in my life I'd been attracted to someone completely different in appearance from Mitzi. Mostly it was Theresa's feminine way of expressing warmth that I loved. And her smile was clear and real.

Up to the time Theresa came into my life I'd been going through a phase of dating one woman after the other. And somewhere through all those one-nighters of booze and beds I seemed to have come to the following absurd conclusion: Mother was Jewish; she rejected me. Mitzi was Jewish; she rejected me. So, Jewish women were fickle and I'd best pursue a Nordic-gentile type. The fact that Sylvia and I had been happy together didn't count. I remember convincing myself that Sylvia wouldn't have become ill with cancer if she hadn't married a reject like me.

By the time Theresa came to me to have her long blonde locks trimmed I was already attending a Catholic church, studying catechism and preparing for baptism. "After all," one priest told me, "our blessed Savior was Jewish."

I can remember clearly that of all the history the church had to offer, the part that I took to easily was the Virgin Mary. The Holy Mother. A mother at last. And one who wouldn't reject me. And the tall slender statues of Mary didn't look like any short, round Jewish mother I'd ever known. So I thought Mary had to be different.

"Mary was a good Jewish mother," I told one priest. He

agreed happily. And I had happy thoughts of Mary feeding Jesus chicken soup, and Jesus being bar mitzvahed, and I could see him at age thirteen reading from the Torah in the temple. And I recall wondering for the first time, and many times since, why Jesus left his tribe, knowing he stood a good chance of being nailed to a cross. Then, I wondered if he had an aunt like Mitzi. And I'd begun to have second thoughts about converting until I found out that Theresa was Catholic. And she was a splendid woman. So, what the hell, why not become a Catholic.

Theresa and I were married. And we'd planned that in a few months we would get my daughter Rachelle. For a while we were happy. And my only desire was to give Theresa everything in the world. But Theresa didn't want the world. And when it struck her that hairdressing would keep me around women (something that did not for some reason occur to her before we were married) she became unhappy. Especially, when I worked overtime.

Until Theresa came to San Francisco she'd spent her life on her parents' farm in West Branch, Michigan. Her whole life was her parents, her sisters and a brother, school, farm, church, and her job with the telephone company. She brought her stable pattern to San Francisco with her. And though I'd told her that I'd been in trouble with the law, it didn't seem to matter. And neither did the fact that we came from completely different cultural and religious backgrounds. None of it mattered—not until we were married.

Her parents were hardworking farmers. She had been accustomed to sharing responsibilities all her life. And when I refused to let her lift a finger to even dust the apartment she became frustrated. "I'm not a toy doll, Irwin," she'd complain. But I refused to listen. I chose and bought her clothes. Styled her hair to suit my tastes, and even tried to tell her she was nuts to not enjoy lox and bagels and cream cheese. "It's not raw fish," I'd say, "it's smoked raw fish. There's a difference!"

Theresa was becoming increasingly unhappy. And after

one good argument, for fear of being rejected again I got a job as a sales representative for Joy Hair Preparations Manufacturers. No more beauty salons. And no more being around women, though Theresa needn't have been concerned. I was too immersed in shaping her my way to have anything to do with other women. And for fear of rejection I gave up asking for lox and cream cheese in the house. I became a closet lox-eater. When I came home with lox on my breath, she didn't complain. But she had become concerned about the smell of too much booze. "Irwin, I wish you would come home to drink. I worry about you. You might get hurt."

"Well, I leave the car home. So, I can't get hurt. Or hurt anyone else."

"Maybe I just want you to share something with me besides our bed."

"Well, I think I'm drinking kind of heavy lately because I know it's time for us to try to get Rachelle. And Mrs. Kavetsky hasn't answered my letters."

"Let's go down to Los Angeles and see what we can do about getting her."

The time had come to face the situation.

It was a horrible scene. Mrs. Kavetsky told Theresa that as far as she was concerned Rachelle had only one mother. And that so long as she had legal custody of Rachelle, it would take a court battle to get her. Then, Mrs. Kavetsky said to me in front of Theresa, "So, Irwin, have you tried to kill yourself lately—or maybe rob a bank lately—or maybe a whole bunch of banks." It was her way of letting me know what a court battle would be like—if there were a court battle.

Yes. I was angry. But I stuffed my anger. Yes. I was disappointed. But I stuffed my disappointment. No. I did not have the courage to fight. Theresa put her arm in mine. We walked away from the Kavetsky house to our car, got in and drove off. "We'll have a child," Theresa said.

"I know, honey. I know."

Joy Hair Chemicals decided to give me a promotion and

transfer me to Chicago. And I could have a month with pay
to get settled. It was nearly Christmas and Theresa was happy because it would give her a chance to spend the holidays
with her folks in West Branch, Michigan. And it would give
her family an opportunity to meet me.

Making plans for the trip was among our more pleasant
moments. We even got rid of our old car and were planning
to buy a new one in Michigan.

Finally the day came. And we were on our way to spend
the holidays with Theresa's family. We'd decided that since
we had plenty of time we would take a Pullman train and see
the country. It was a marvelous trip. In just a few days after
leaving sunny California, we arrived in Detroit. It was snow-
ing, and by the time we arrived in the small farm community
of Theresa's home, a blizzard was on us.

Now I could see through my own eyes the farm where
Theresa was born. Typical rural Americana in a setting of
snow and Christmas tinsel complete with potbelly stove and
a Christmas tree. Her father—a tall, muscular gentleperson
who'd worked the farm all his life except for short periods
when he ran a horse and wagon on Mackinaw Island for the
tourists—looked at me in squinting disbelief. "Can you handle a beer?" he asked generously, but sounding a bit dubious.

Theresa's mother—who had raised six children "without
back talk," and taught school in a one-room schoolhouse,
"without back talk"—had to take her glasses off, wipe them
on her apron, slip them back, slowly, up the bridge of her
nose, so she could get proper focus on me. This done, she
removed her glasses again, and cleared her throat. "I hear
you're a beauty operator." She said. And cleared her throat
again. "I also hear you're one of those Jewish people."

"Well," I said, looking around for Theresa who had disappeared into the kitchen. "I was Jewish. But I'm a Catholic
now."

"Can't be both. You're one or the other. Besides you have a
Jewish nose."

"Jesus was a Jew, you know." I began to sweat.

"Sure, I know. But you hung him up," she said.

"Not me." I corrected. "I didn't hang anyone."

"Same thing."

"Well, Theresa and I are going to raise our children to be Catholics."

"Why—'shamed of being Jewish?"

Then, Theresa's father saved me. "Leave him alone," he told his wife. "I met a lot of Jewish fellas in the First World War—all worked in the supply depot. They were okay. Besides. He's our son-in-law now. Our daughter loves him. That's enough." I couldn't figure out if he meant it was enough for him that Theresa apparently loved me, or if he thought it was "enough" interrogation.

And, that's the way the holiday went: Theresa's father testing my tolerance for beer. And, her mother testing my tolerance. And I could tolerate. At least, Theresa had good parents. They cared about their kids. Which is more than I could say for my own parents.

Theresa had a married sister, Doris, who lived in Flint, Michigan, with her husband Albert. And somehow we decided that we could rent a house near her sister's; of course, I would have to quit my job and find another. "But that shouldn't be any problem." Everyone agreed. Everyone except Albert who felt sorry for me.

So, I quit my job and found work as a furniture salesman. Now I was out of the beauty business. Everyone was happy. Still, no one except Albert in Theresa's family took to me. But Theresa was happier than she'd been for a long while. And she stayed happy until she got pregnant.

"I don't want a baby." She cried all through her pregnancy. And I felt she meant that she didn't want my baby. Even so, I looked forward to our coming event. And, then our daughter Terri was born. I was ecstatic.

And somehow I felt older than my twenty-seven years. "We're going back to California," I told Theresa. And go back to California we did.

"I am going to be a hairdresser again." I told Theresa. And go back to dressing hair I did. And we made our adjustments.

Five years had passed since Sylvia's death. And, five years had passed since I'd committed a crime. And though my life was filled with my new family I could not get my daughter Rachelle out of my mind.

During the period that we lived in Palo Alto, Theresa and I decided that my mother should know her granddaughter Terri. Problems began to arise. And I swallowed a lot of bad memories. It was especially painful to me whenever we saw my mother and stepfather. I would see my father's ruby ring—on my stepfather's thick, hairy finger. The ring my mother accused me of stealing. I tried to tell myself that someday mother would make things right. And at least tell me she was sorry. But she didn't. She hasn't. Not ever.

I styled hair at Klugman's Department Store. And work kept me going smoothly. I'd been working a great deal of overtime. Mainly because my mother had been coming around frequently—and it upset me.

It was one of those very busy days at the salon, where lunch had to go to hell and women were pacing around in their curlers crying to be combed out so they could "go home and fix dinner." The kind of a day when I would least expect fire-green eyes and wispy bangs and tiny titties to come into my life. But nevertheless there she was. And she was carrying a brown paper sack. "I'm Yvonne—I brought you some lunch because I don't have an appointment and I want you to cut my hair. My friend, Emily, recommended you. How do you like your coffee?"

"Don't have time for coffee. And as you can see I'm really busy," I said apologetically. But I wanted to know this green-eyed lady. "Look. Tell you what. Just stand close by and I'll work you in. But don't wander. Stay close."

She walked right up close to me. I almost dropped my comb. "This close enough?" she smiled.

It was close enough. And, finally I'd cut her hair. "How about a coffee?" I said. "I have time now and I want to know you."

We had an affair. And, yes, we spent every possible moment
together. Sometimes only an hour. But they were hours filled
with Khalil Gibran, the Brownings' letters, talk of life on
other planets, and Frank Sinatra singing "You are my
Special Angel." And I believed her when she said, "It's got to
be yours. My husband had a vasectomy a long time ago,
because it's too dangerous for me to have children. I could
die. I'm scared. And besides him—you're it. So what are we
going to do?"

"Do you care about me?" I asked.

"You mean love you? Yes, I do. I love you and care about
you. But I'm scared."

"I just don't understand why you didn't ask me to use
precautions. I'm going to speak to your husband."

"I didn't ask you to use precautions because I want your
baby. I want to marry you."

"But you need to be aborted before it's too late. You said
yourself, you could die from pregnancy."

In nineteen-fifty-eight abortions of any kind were illegal.
But it was my responsibility. And something had to be done.
"I've got to have a talk with your husband."

"I'm scared, Irwin. He'll kill us both."

"Maybe. But I doubt it. And we can't just disappear. Your
life is at stake. And mine? Well, it's been a strange life
anyway." I was remembering how Theresa's mother had insisted that I couldn't be a Catholic because I had a "Jewish
nose." I wondered if Jesus had a "Jewish nose" and an aunt
like Mitzi, and I remember wishing for a wife who would
share my love for lox and cream cheese.

Fortified with a few straight belts of bourbon, I confronted
her husband in their living room. He wore his blonde hair in
a crewcut. And his red eyes showed tired signs. He, as it
turned out, was more concerned about his image at work.
"Everyone knows I've been cut. I'll be a laughing stock," he
whined.

And listening to his whining, I began to understand how

Yvonne and I had been thrown together. He did want her aborted. Not because she could lose her life, but because of his own embarrassment. He didn't talk about Yvonne's life at all. Sure. I could understand his anger. His hurt. And maybe he wanted her dead. Who knows. But a human life takes priority over anyone's ego or embarrassment.

"Yvonne needs to be aborted. And I'm taking her out of town to get it done."

"Will you bring her back to me?" he whimpered. Hearing him whimper like that nauseated me. But I knew I had all the cards. And I played them.

"If she wants to come back. But right now every moment counts. I just hope we can find someone competent to do it. Listen, if you don't mind . . . you have two cars—and I don't want to leave my wife without a car. Can Yvonne and I take one of yours?"

Now that Yvonne's husband had been dealt with I had to tell Theresa. "Don't come back," she said coolly.

So, Yvonne and I left Palo Alto and went to Los Angeles. I hadn't the vaguest idea where I'd get the money for an abortion. Theresa and I had a little money saved and a joint checking account. But I didn't want to deprive my family for my mistake. I didn't touch that money. Yvonne had a bank credit card and some cash—but nowhere near enough cash for an illegal abortion. And it had been a long time since I stole. I really didn't feel up to stealing.

For a while, our problem was bearable because Yvonne and I enjoyed being together. We had rented a room at the Hollywood-Roosevelt Hotel on Yvonne's credit card— actually the card was in her husband's name so I signed the register according to the name on the credit card. The hotel clerk was busy and didn't compare signatures too carefully. What little cash we did have on hand would have to be used for the research expense involved in locating an abortionist. "I'd better call my boss," I said to Yvonne. "I'm due at work tomorrow—and I'm booked solid. Got to give him a chance to spread my work around. Also, I want to ask him for a loan.

And I want to be sure I have a job when I get back.''

"No loan. No job. There's already gossip. Can't afford scandal. Not good for business. But you do have some pay coming—want me to send it to you?''

"Take my pay and . . . and send it to my wife. In fact, I'd appreciate it if you make the check out in her name." By the time I'd hung up the receiver my decision was made. I'd steal. It would take a bit of planning—not too much though, not enough time.

It was when Yvonne and I were readying to go out to dinner. I was watching Yvonne undress to shower, delighting at the shape of her tiny titties. Mitzi's name popped into my head. Mitzi lived in Los Angeles—I knew where—and I could ask her for money. So, at dinner I excused myself and went to a pay phone.

"I'm sorry, Irwin. I just don't have it," Mitzi said. And she sounded in a hurry to get off the phone.

"Mitzi. Can I bring Yvonne to meet you?"

"Irwin, for both of our sakes—stay out of my life."

That night, back in our hotel room, when Yvonne fell asleep I rifled her purse. I didn't know what I'd find that would be of any use except her checkbook. But there were a few more credit cards and a deposit book. I remembered my surprise when I saw a checking balance of four-thousand dollars. I formulated my plan, and removed one check from the back of Yvonne's checkbook and slipped it in my billfold. I still had the bank credit card Yvonne had given me and I decided to leave the other credit cards in her purse. I stayed up all night, in the bathroom, practicing her husband's signature; I would have to be more careful with the signature than when we registered for our room. By morning I had the signature down pat. And I had to move quickly so as not to lose the feel of the style.

Yvonne was still asleep and I nudged her. "I'm going out to see about finding a doctor for you. Just make a few calls. Be back in an hour or so.''

"No. Come to bed. I need you." Yvonne always "needed"

me. There was never a moment when she didn't. She made me feel important. And I loved her for it. But, I had to move quickly. And bed with Yvonne was never a quick trip. So I said, "I need you, too. But I'm worried. And unless we take care of this now—well, you understand."

"Okay," she protested. "But don't forget. You owe me."

"Good morning," I smiled to the banker. "My wife and I are on an extended vacation and something urgent has come up. I'd like to cash a check for two thousand dollars."

"Certainly, sir. Do you have our bank credit card with you?"

"Yes. I do." I handed him the card.

"Oh. You're one of our gold-carders. That should be no problem at all. Now if you don't mind would you make out your check."

My stomach knotted. Here was the test. The signature. "Certainly." I said removing the check from my billfold. "Always keep a check or two in my billfold. Don't like to carry a checkbook. Gets lost too easily. Can't tell who might pick it up." I made out the check.

"Oh, right you are. Can't be too careful these days," he agreed. "Now I'll just call your bank in Palo Alto and put a 'hold' on the amount. Of course I'll have to get time and charges for the long distance call. But we'll bill that to your account."

I hadn't counted on the bank officer calling the bank in Palo Alto. And I panicked, inwardly. But there was no way to stop him. Not unless I wanted him to get suspicious of me. And so far it was a pleasant transaction. At least as far as he was concerned. "Certainly. I understand," I said, trying to maintain my cool. "Those damned phone bills can really add up. My wife thinks I have a bottomless income the way she uses that phone."

The banker picked up the phone saying to me, "Your wife too—huh. Oh well, all part of life . . . Excuse me . . ."

The call went smoothly. But I still wanted to get out of that bank as quickly as possible without creating undue motion. I looked at my watch. "Ten-thirty. I have an eleven o'clock appointment on Western and Sunset. Is that very far?" I knew it was—but I had to keep my out-of-town image.

"Oh, not very," he said. "Let me get your money for you. It won't take long."

While the banker was gone I kept thinking that maybe whoever it was he spoke to in the bank branch in Palo Alto had said something that might have tipped him off to me, and that he was really out of sight calling the law. But, he returned in a few minutes, counted out ten one-hundred-dollar bills and gave me the rest in fifties and twenties. "Here you are. Two-thousand dollars. Would you like an envelope?"

"Yes, I would like an envelope," I said relieved. And that familiar surge of power swept through me. I was reminded of that day I robbed Jim LaFamento's bank.

Yvonne was in bed reading *The Prophet* when I returned. "Sure glad I took Gibran along," she said, feigning a pout. "He keeps me company even if you don't."

"Just like all the others," I said, trying to conceal my excitement. "A man goes away for an hour and comes back to find his woman in bed with another man."

"You sound jealous," Yvonne teased. "Come on—take your clothes off—come to bed. It's only eleven o'clock in the morning. Haven't stayed in bed this late for years."

I got undressed, hung my clothes in the closet and checked the envelope of money in my inside jacket pocket. "Yvonne," I lied, "I went to see an old friend of mine. Got some money he'd owed me for a long time. Now we don't have to worry about money for a doctor. From what I can determine it shouldn't cost more than seven or eight hundred. And now I've got more than enough."

"Don't want to talk about it right now. Come to bed."

I got in bed beside her and slipped my arms around her. I noticed that her lips were drained of color and trembling.

"Yvonne," I said gently, "I love you."

"Irwin, I love you too." She began to cry. "But I'm frightened. Really scared. I'm frightened more than . . ."

"Shhh, darling," I said trying to soothe her. "I'll be by you. I won't desert you."

"I know," she sobbed, "you are so beautiful. I want so much to give you a baby."

I was touched. Deeply. No one had ever said that to me. Not even Sylvia. Oh, Sylvia was happy about being pregnant with Rachelle. But she never said those words to me. And Theresa only complained about being pregnant. Though after our daughter Terri was born, Theresa fell completely in love with her. Yet, she never told me she wanted my baby.

Now, Yvonne had said it. Yvonne with the fire-green eyes. Yvonne with the soul of a poet. Yvonne with the tenderness of an autumn breeze. Yvonne with the imagination to carry us to the edge of the universe. "No, not the edge of the universe, Irwin," she'd say softly, gazing into my eyes. "The universe is like the soul. No edge. It's like a Mobius strip—you can start a journey from the Milky Way and walk along the stars—blindfolded and, eventually wind up right back in the Milky Way. Without even a map!"

I asked her if she'd ever heard of the planet Lam. She said she hadn't but that didn't mean anything because she was "Spanish and French," and Lam probably was not in a territory she'd traveled yet. Then she laughed. A tender, gentle laugh of hot sun and cold brook waters. And all this feminine beauty was wanting a baby with me. I thought of just having robbed. I thought of Zayda. And his roses and peaches. And I remembered Mitzi's planet Lam. And Coney Island. And I wanted to be with my daughters. I longed for the planet Earth.

I pulled Yvonne's head close to mine hoping she would not know that the tears now flowing from my own soul had been prompted by my own feelings of guilt and remorse, and complete self-loathing. And as my tears mingled with Yvonne's I sensed that she too had thoughts other than our own immediate problem. Perhaps she too wanted to return to the Earth, and that it seemed to her terribly distant from the Milky Way, just as the planet Lam did for me. But instead of talking about our individual tormenting thoughts, we held each other close and said "I love you." And my thoughts turned to the money in my jacket pocket and Mexico.

VIII

We chose Ciudad Obregon, Mexico, after a Mexican bartender in San Diego said, "Very good doctor . . . very good care . . . very reasonable . . . I would take my own wife to him." He scribbled the doctor's name on the back of a cocktail napkin. The bartender also told us to be certain to mention his name to him. But he didn't write his own name down. And by the time we arrived in beautiful Obregon we'd forgotten it.

It was a hundred-and-six degrees of humid heat in the shade. We managed to find a nice air-conditioned room in a decent motel—a motel frequented by Mexican businessmen. In the late fifites, Ciudad Obregon, even with its palm-tree-lined boulevards and wild parakeets was not a tourist attraction. Even today, because of the heat and humidity, it is not among the most favored by tourists. Because of the lack of American influence, there is very little English spoken there. But the people were warm and hospitable to us. They strained beyond limits to understand us. And by the time we located the doctor we had made new friends.

The doctor's office was not unlike that of a general practitioner here in the United States. The small waiting room was crowded. And the only communication we had with the other people who were waiting to see the doctor was our mutual smiles.

Finally, a dark-eyed young girl dressed in a white nurse's uniform motioned us into the inner office. *"Pase, pase, por favor,"* she smiled. And led us into the doctor's examining room—where we were seated.

"I don't have the opportunity to practice much in English," the doctor said. "But, you say a man in San Diego told you to come here?"

"Yes. A very nice man. Right, Yvonne?"

"Oh yes. Very nice," Yvonne agreed, and smiled at the doctor.

"Well, no matter. Tell me," the doctor said. "What is your problem?"

After discussing the "problem," and trying earnestly to discourage us, the doctor agreed to operate on Yvonne.

"But," he warned, "I will not do it unless you agree to stay at least two weeks after the operation. I must keep watch on her. And you must stay where I say—a friend of mine, Guillermo Valdez and his family."

We agreed. And the operation was done. Three-hundred dollars. That included the doctor's daily visits. I offered him more money. But he became offended. So, I dropped the subject of money. But I did offer the marvelous family we stayed with whatever they wanted. But they took only enough money for *abarrotes* (groceries). And cared for Yvonne and me as though we were part of their own family.

Yvonne recovered rapidly. And during her recovery, Guillermo Valdez and I became *hermanos*, brothers. He tried to teach me Spanish. But, until my last trip to Obregon some years later, I was a slow learner.

All went well. And Yvonne and I left Obregon and returned to Los Angeles. And checked in to a different hotel. We wanted a few more days together before we returned to Palo Alto to settle our affairs. We'd talked about divorcing our spouses. And we talked about our future marriage. But, I did not tell her about that when she said, "I'm going to call home and tell my husband to get ready for a divorce."

I knew if she called he would tell her about the hole in their bank account. But I kept quiet about it. And waited nervously for the results of the phone call. So, Yvonne picked up the receiver on our room phone and put a call through to her husband. After she'd talked to him for a few moments of mostly "Yes, I understands," she handed the phone to me. "He wants to talk to you."

"Me?" I said taking the phone. "Hello."

"Hello my ass," he said. "You weren't satisfied just screwing Yvonne, son-of-a-bitch, you had to fuck me too—don't answer—I haven't told her—and I assume you haven't—

because I know her well enough to know that she'd never be a party to stealing . . . screwing maybe, but not stealing. Anyway I'll make a deal with—are you listening?"

"Yes." What choice did I have?

"I want my wife back. Crazy—huh?"

"No, not really. I can understand." I sensed what was coming next.

"Anyway, bastard, little-Jesus—I won't prosecute you for forgery if you leave her life—and don't come back. Is it a deal—or do I call the cops?"

I became depressed and angry simultaneously. That son-of-a-bitch wanted her back to torment her—I knew that. And I hated him for it. He was even willing not send me to jail for the privilege of having her within spitting distance, while he whined "you almost made me a laughing stock." Or maybe he loved her. Maybe. Whatever it was he wanted, he wanted it badly enough to pay for it. "Can I think about it for a few days?" I said.

Yvonne paced around the room—curiosity gripped her—she kept whispering, "What's he saying," all the while I was on the phone.

"What do you call a 'few days'?" he asked.

"Oh, about three."

"That's what you've got. Exactly. You can have her for three more days—then I expect you to tell her that you don't want to marry her—that it was bullshit all along. Got that?"

"I got it. Goodbye." I hung up without asking him if he wanted to talk further with Yvonne.

"What did he have to say to you," Yvonne asked.

"Oh, just talked about the embarrassment we caused him."

"Well, we did that. But he never cared about embarrassing anyone. Not me. . . ."

"What about you. Did he give you a bad time?"

"Didn't even ask how I felt. Well, I can't blame him for that. But he said if I tried to get a divorce he had proof of what I did and he'd get everything. And I never told you, Ir-

win, because our relationship goes beyond material things—
but we have a lot of property . . . a bunch. What about you.
Do you stand to lose much—financially . . . I already know
how hurt you are about not seeing your daughter."

"That's what hurts. You're right. But I should have
thought about that before you and I became involved. Financially . . . not much. I'd leave it for Theresa and Terri
anyway. I can always make it. Anyway we've got to go back
to Palo Alto to settle things."

The next two days, my mind became a virtual battlefield. I
didn't want to go to jail. And I didn't want to lose Yvonne. I
had about eight hundred dollars left from the two thousand
and I figured if need be I could set up another bank—only
this time I'd be a little more original. I'd do a fantastic job.
But, I didn't want to. Not really. And, Theresa had already
said I couldn't come home. Mitzi said not to call her again.
Fuck it. I'll tell Yvonne the truth. And I did. It was the first
time I'd heard her swear. "Why that dirty son-of-a-bitch.
Why that's blackmail—holding jail over your head in order
to get me back. Irwin, you were stupid. I'd have gotten the
money. I have it. My own money. All you would have had to
do was ask me . . . No, you wouldn't have asked me—not you.

"But you lied to me. Though I understand, a lie is a lie.
Well, you'd best do as he says. Take me home."

I took Yvonne home. Stopped in front of her door, handed
her back her car keys, kissed her on the cheek and said, "I
love you." She didn't answer. She just opened the door and
went in the house.

I turned away. Went to see Theresa. "I told you not to
come back."

"I want to tell you I'm sorry. And you are the only stabiliz-
ing factor in my life. No. I'm not staying. Just want to give
you some money. See Terri. Then get the rest of my things
together and go."

"Where are you going?"

"Don't really know. But I'll send money for you and Terri.

I can give you four hundred for now. Not much. But I'll send more—soon."

"Would you like to stay for dinner?"

"No. I don't believe so. It would just make leaving harder. I can't stay. Not now."

"No, Irwin. I don't want you to stay. I can't live with what you've done. But I love you."

"Maybe in another lifetime," I said.

"Whoever taught you this 'other lifetime' stuff?" Theresa asked. She was annoyed.

"My grandfather. Why?"

"What about the here and now?"

"He told me about that too. And that's why I should be on my way. There's some 'here and now' to take care of." So, I turned my back to Theresa, Terri, Rachelle and I even turned my back on myself.

IX

Goodbye, Theresa. Goodbye, Terri. Goodbye, Yvonne. A voice from many lives past beckons me. A voice I must follow at any cost. Chasing a voice could become expensive. But if my money runs out I can always bilk a bank . . . become a master of illusions and thievery.

Among the important points of creating an illusion, I had learned, was to have a "front," a place to work—a place to work that itself was a legal front.

Without particular reason I headed for San Bernardino. And managed to locate the master of all confidence men, Doc Prudent. He was promoting charities there. And he did this using "boiler room" techniques. A "boiler room" is an office equipped with telephones and people that know how to talk convincingly on those phones: "Hello, Mr. Lollipop, this is MacPherson calling for the Ladies of the Light—you know— the gals that spread light and cheer to folks around. Anyway, Mr. Lollipop, you being a businessman and a staunch supporter of your community, I know you'd be interested in driving a bus load of black kids to our picnic . . . Oh, I'm sorry, I didn't think you'd be so busy. Tell you what, you can help anyway, and still get a good feeling. We can send a bunch of black kids to that picnic for just forty dollars . . . spend more than that on your girl friend in Reno (ha ha). So, what I'll do is send one of our ladies over to see you; she'll have an official receipt. And listen, you don't get to keep her there. She's the prettiest one we have. So send her on to us, you rascal, you . . . Okay? . . .forty dollars—just make your check out to the Ladies of the Light—L-I-G-H-T. And in case you're not in, who will you leave the check with? Emma? Oh, yeah, Emma—how is Emma these days? Listen, I'll spread the word around to the Ladies of the Light . . . can't tell when they can do you a favor back . . ."

Absurd, you say? Well, there are damned few businessmen around the world—that's right, I said, "world"—who haven't at one time received a phone call like that. And they do write forty-dollar checks. Not much? Well, multiply that by ten people working the phones, four hours a day making on the average of forty calls each. That's four-hundred calls a day. A phone-room filled with "pros" can average a fifty percent close. So, say two-hundred calls at forty dollars a crack. That's a lot of smackers in anybody's language. Eight-thousand dollars a day—collected by "one of the Ladies" that you don't "get to keep. . . . ."

Twenty-five percent or two-thousand dollars of the eight-thousand goes into "sales commissions." That's two-hundred dollars a day per salesperson. Ten percent for the "Ladies of the Light," that's eight-hundred dollars a day for them. Anyway, the promoter winds up with the daily balance of five-thousand two-hundred dollars or more. Not a bad day's pay. From that money the promoter pays the office and phone expense.

And, Doc Prudent ran these rooms all over the state of California.

There are lots of promoters around the world like Doc. And I've worked for most of them. But not all are willing to supply phony identification for a man on the run. He did. He used it as leverage to keep the best salespeople.

Anyway, I met Doc. And he introduced me to his "manager." I had a job in San Bernardino. A job. Phony identification and money in my pocket.

Next I was off to a spiritualist church. And after a good look around I found my new ladylove, Rene; tiny titties, dark hair, fire-green eyes. And, for a while there was bliss and I had feelings of love. We'd have seances. We performed ritual dances around bowls of incense, and I would tell her stories about my mystic grandfather. Rene would read the crystal ball for me. And I'd promise to show her the secrets of the ages. We'd even get married. Why not?

And after the marriage, I'd set up a bank and go to work. Rene had no idea, none of them did.

In San Bernardino, Rene and I had a quiet wedding ceremony and a few quiet weeks together. Doc was getting pissed that I wasn't showing up at the office. He threatened to fire me. But by that time I had set a "business account" in the Franklin Bank on Fourth and Y Streets with five hundred dollars from a two-thousand-dollar bankroll I had managed to save from my earnings in Doc's "boiler room." I was planning a take. Timing and details were critical.

I rented an office for a front and had a phone installed. Then opened my "business account" under the name of "Jack King" doing business as "Surprises Unlimited." I remember telling the banker that my business was planning unique surprises for any occasion. "I wish you luck," said the banker, "let me know if I can do anything for you. Your printed checks will be ready in just a few days. Shall I send them to you?"

"No, thanks. I'll drop by for them."

In the next few days under three different names, I.D. for each, I opened three more "business accounts" in three different banks—for one hundred dollars each. I then proceeded, LaFamento style, to work the wheel of fortune by depositing checks from one bank into another until I had all four banks spinning with thousands of dollars. These accounts looked tremendous on paper—one check covering another. And I knew all was okay until I drew cash from any one of the accounts over the actual cash I have on deposit. Once I drew cash I had three banking days from the day of withdrawal in which to disappear. I could start my venture on a Friday in San Bernardino, work through to Sunday and be in Mexico City or New York or Milwaukee before my wheel of fortune fell off its axle.

To make my checks impressive, I bought a desk top typewriter and a mechanical marvel known as a "check protector," or "check writer"—a machine that prints perforated dollar amounts and the legend "INSURED," "REGISTERED," or "BONDED," along the "sum" line of a check.

The purpose of a check protector is to prevent slippery scamps from altering checks. But anyone can purchase a check protector—even scamps. Anyone who's willing to risk going to jail can open a bank account with two hundred dollars, and with one of these marvelous money machines crank out a crooked caper that could, with careful long-range planning, net millions of dollars.

When I picked my checks up from the banks I wasn't thinking of stealing millions. I only wanted enough to enable me to travel comfortably for a while. With the wheel of fortune operating properly each of my four bank accounts showed a balance of five-thousand dollars.

It was Thursday evening. In the privacy of my office, just like an ordinary businessman, I sat at my desk figuring the payroll. I reasoned that a reimbursement check of one-hundred-forty-three dollars and thirty-eight cents to a salesman for expenses would not arouse suspicion. I set the buttons on my check protector and cranked out thirty checks for one-hundred-forty-three dollars and thirty-eight cents each.

Each of the sets of I.D. Doc supplied came complete with credit cards. "Don't attempt to use the credit cards for anything except identification," Doc cautioned. "and don't use them in the stores they're issued from. They're perfect replicas, but worthless for purchases. Remember that!"

I had six sets of identification. I chose one set made out in the name of "Charles Daverson," and typed that name on the "Pay to" line of my payroll checks.

If I made an average purchase of forty dollars with each check, by the time I had cashed all the checks I would be three thousand dollars richer. Then I figured I would withdraw two-thousand-two-hundred-forty dollars from each of my "business accounts." That would give me an additional nine thousand for my trip. I could have pulled the total scam on the banks alone and not bothered with the payroll checks, but I remember feeling nervous over the slightest chance of suspicion that I could create by almost depleting my bank balances. And by leaving a balance in the bank I drew my paychecks on, a suspicious store manager could call the bank and check to see if the record showed enough money on deposit to cover the check. I knew that too many calls to the bank could also arouse suspicion, so I decided to work the bulk of the stores when the banks were closed.

That evening, before I left the office, I wrote "Charles Daverson" over and over until I felt comfortable with it. One slip, such as signing my right name, could mean the end of the caper.

I thumbed through the stack of phony paychecks imagining them to be spendable cash. Then I inspected each check down to the smallest detail. I read each aloud, slowly: Surprises Unlimited . . . Four-seventy-one Y street, San Bernardino, California . . . Pay to: Charles Daverson . . . Sum of One-hundred-forty-three dollars and thirty-eight cents . . . $143.38 . . . Authorized signature: Jack King . . . Expense reimbursement.

I remember carrying everything out of the office that night. I remember putting the check protector, typewriter, and I.D. I wouldn't have use for under an Army surplus blanket in the trunk of my car. I remember removing the batteries from a flashlight I had kept on the front seat of the car and replacing the batteries with the payroll checks which I rolled to fit inside the flashlight. I remember feeling a bit sad as I drove home. This would be my last few days with Rene.

Friday, at one in the afternoon, when the banks were crowded and the tellers were busy with end-of-the-week transactions, I visited each one of my four banks and withdrew two-thousand-two-hundred-fifty dollars from each. Then I proceeded to hit the chain stores. Never a "Mom and Pop" operation—the big companies were insured.

By Sunday sundown, I had hit the four banks, some clothing and shoe stores, and numerous supermarkets. The trunk and back seat of my car was filled with food which I couldn't use, or bring to my ladylove because I was leaving; and along with the food I had new shoes, cameras, radios, and liquor.

I worked hard. And by the time I counted my cash I had

twelve-thousand dollars—most of the cash came from the banks.

I tried giving the radios and cameras and shoes and liquor away. But couldn't. People were too suspicious of giveaways. And I didn't want a trunk full of crap. Why? Well, in case I got stopped for a traffic violation and the cops decided to pull a search and saw all those radios, cameras and liquor— I'd get hauled in on suspicion. That's why. So, what did I do with all that glitter. Well, if you go to the city dump in San Bernardino you may find it. But, that was over twenty years ago. And maybe it wasn't San Bernardino. It could have been a city on the planet Lam.

I left San Bernardino, and Rene. And Doc Prudent.

For twenty years before I went to prison, my priorities were potato *lotkes* and pussy; chicken *kreplach* soup, wine-tasting, Eugene O'Neill and Ravel and sopping up the sights from San Francisco to Ciudad Obregon. Occasionally I'd bilk a bank to support my lifestyle. On rare occasions my bank jobs were interrupted because providence would present me with a lithe, long-legged, intelligent female who could fix potato *lotkes* and screw like an acrobat and who had a healthy divorce settlement or a career that scooped up a sizeable paycheck. Then, bank job go to hell.

And if she just so happened to own a decent collection of records and good books, and if by chance she happened to dig interpreting the pictures on tarot cards, gaze mysteriously into crystal balls, work up astrology charts, practice ceremonial witchcraft, study the Cabala or any of the myriad of occult and esoteric sciences with a smattering of Aleister Crowley and Ernest Holmes thrown in for an evening's speculation, I just may want to move in with her. What I would do is play up the fact that I was the direct grandson of a cabalist who taught me everything he'd learned from the ancient mystic Hebrew books just before he went on to his next life. Then I'd let it be known to her that it would be no problem at all for me to stay over, "Just a few days. Enough time to show you grandfather's method of quickly extricating karma. Then, I must be getting on to more earthly business . . ."

It may not be the most direct, but for me the occult was a sure way to pussy—and a roof over my head when my "earthly business" happened to be hiding from the cops.

See: The cops figured I was running alone. So, hooking up to a cult nut was good cover for me. And I did in fact meet some ultralovely fortune-tellers, and women who professed to be witches. So when an aspiring witch offered a potion I'd casually mention that I was a student of black magic and that wouldn't it be a blast to put our potions together.

Where would I meet them? In spiritualist churches from San Francisco to New York City. If I had to, I'd marry them. I'd stick around until I felt things getting too hot, then move on. Getting naked with an attractive crystal ball-gazer, reciting a few chants over sandalwood smoke and candle light, and screwing the night away is a hell of a lot more fun and more desirable than sitting in a jail cell. Even if it meant marriage. So, that's the way it was. Cops chasing me from every direction, and running close behind the cops were a half-a-dozen irate, disenchanted, crystal ball-gazers. The two groups had one thing in common. They all wanted to stuff me—balls first—into the slammer. But for twenty years, trying to pin me down was harder than spreading butter on the rising sun.

X

When time in my cell in Folsom Prison became almost unbearable, I thought of Jennifer. And I wished it could have been just "friends," as she'd suggested on the plane. And I'd wished I hadn't been on that plane at all.

My plans in Dallas hadn't worked. If they had, I'd have probably been in prison in Texas. And that, from what I hear—chain gangs and all—would have been worse.

I've met odd people in my travels, but never anyone like Jack Frazer and his wife, Cindy. Both college grads, both sophisticated. He was vice-president in charge of marketing for a large drug chain. And she? She had the kind of soft blonde loveliness that goes with an executive's salary. Figure of a fashion model. Dressed smartly, not ostentatious. Never said a word out of place, and the soft caress of her voice held a subtle hint of excitement.

Jack was a diplomat. Tall, slim and radiated a public relations smile. He boasted of being "expanded in my thinking. After all, I do get wrapped up in my work, and I don't expect Cindy to sit at home."

I met them at the Science of Mind church (I always met my "marks" in church) in Dallas at a Sunday afternoon coffee social. I had bought an expensive suit for the occasion. Just part of my investment, along with sport clothes and an expensive furnished apartment, but my budget wouldn't allow for a car. I needed cash to entertain my marks and set up accounts or buy a couple of shares of stock—just for flash. It takes money to make money. And that applies even if you're going to steal it—especially if you're going to steal it.

And, I'd gone through exacting details for the take. Including a hair job from one of those hair-weaving salons. For four-hundred dollars, I had a crop of silver-white hair— Princeton cut—woven to my existing, already sparse hair. Weaving assures that the wig won't fly off in the wind, float away in a swimming pool, or fall off while screwing. I'd tried other kinds of hair pieces—the kind you hang up at night. But one night, I was visiting with a lady who owned a playful cat.

The cat hopped on my shoulder and knocked my hairpiece off. It fell off my lap and on to the floor. The cat sprang on it, dragged it over to a corner of the room, where it proceeded to hunch and stalk around my new wig, as though it was a rat. Did my lady friend laugh? You bet your ass she laughed. All fucking night. After that I decided that even though weave jobs cost a little more, I wasn't going to risk letting another cat do a job on me.

Anyway, there I was having coffee with my new acquaintances, Jack and Cindy. New suit, new hair, and height builders in my shoes. "I'm Irwin," I said introducing myself to Jack and Cindy. "Irwin Altman." Placing solid emphasis on the name Altman hoping it would strike a familiar note. In the past, people knowing my real name asked me if I were related to the department store people. Of course, I'd said no, unless I could use the deception for a gainful purpose. But I wanted to plant that seed firmly in the minds of Jack and Cindy. I had purpose.

"Altman," Jack said, as though trying to remember where he'd heard the name before. "I know," he continued, "any relation to that B. Altman?—the big department store in New York?"

The seed worked. "Uh, no. I'm not," I said, trying to make it sound as though I were concealing the fact that I could very well be. It worked. Jack didn't buy my "No."

He smiled at Cindy and winked. Then smiled at me. "Okay. Sure. Just plain old Altman. If that's the way you want it."

"That's the way, Jack," I said. "For now, anyway. Lots of reasons." My "reasons"? Well, I'd always planned my con games by ear. Basic plan, but open enough to allow for any change necessary. But, I was so intrigued by Jack and Cindy, I had already shut my thinker off.

"Hear that, Cindy?" Jack winked, "we've got another confidence to keep." Jack nudged Cindy's shoulder with his. And smiled out of the corner of his mouth.

Cindy extended a hand to me. "Please to meet you. Irwin, is it?"

"Say," Jack said, "how'd you like to come to a little afternoon party at our home today?"

"Well, it's a little late to go home, change, and find my way to your home for an afternoon party."

"Why go home? Just follow us."

"I'm not driving. Doctor's orders," I lied. As good an excuse as any for not having a car.

"Well, then drive with us. Won't take no for an answer. Heart problem?"

"No. Just nerves."

"Nerves, eh? Our Cindy has a sure cure for frayed nerves. Don't you, honey?" he grinned—a sly grin. It made my skin chill. She just smiled knowingly. And something about the way those two stood together, smiling, and their immediate, warm, chatty attitude, and the way Jack said, "Our Cindy," reminded me of the Geritol commercial couples. Except I got the impression that it wasn't vitamins they were selling. And meeting them at a church social I discounted anything bizarre like an orgy. Not that I wasn't beyond screwing another guy's wife, if circumstance called for it. I could do that without so much as a twinge of conscience. In fact, screwing another man's wife was, for me, more desirable than stealing money.

I made a snap decision. Generally my pattern was to "build" a relationship. Not move too quickly. But on that occasion I can recall assuring myself that it would be harmless to alter the foundation of my operation's method. For two reasons: This was to be the big one, and Jack and Cindy seemed a good point of departure; and . . . the silk-panty quality of Cindy's voice. Besides, I told myself, if they didn't have the money, they sure as shit would know someone who did.

In prison, the sound of a woman's voice is heard only on television or at visits or over guntower loudspeakers when the female guards warn: "You're too close to the walls. Get behind the yellow line." And sometimes in the middle of the night I would call Cindy's voice into my sex fantasies. I had as much variety in my fantasies of sex in prison as I did in reality on the streets. Sometimes I'd call up several memories at the same time. And sometimes I'd remember that Aunt Mitzi had said the do-it-yourself kind of sex could become more pleasurable than the real thing. Bullshit. Maybe it is "less expensive to marry your hand," as some people say in jest, but did you ever try sharing a little joke you heard at work with your hand? Hell, part of my fantasies were conversations with the women I've known. Cindy especially. Because she loved to talk about fantasies, and act them out. "The only rule, is no violence," she'd say.

And I couldn't have a fantasy about Cindy without remembering the afternoon party and the whole crazy costly situation in Dallas. And I couldn't have a fantasy about Cindy without remembering that it was our brief encounter that was to gradually wake me from a long-lived nightmare. A slow awakening. It takes a little time to sweep away the fading fragments of any dream, especially when you want to grab on to a few familiar fragments before they float out of sight, forever, and out of reach. And in prison, I had plenty of time to chase fragments. But, it wasn't until I let the last fragment of Cindy slip away completely, that I could see a child who was left with his pants down because he rolled the dice in a Monopoly game and went directly to jail: Do not pass GO. Do not collect two-hundred dollars . . . But Aunt Mitzi gave me two-hundred dollars—the day she walked away from the game and left me with my pants down . . . only, she didn't pee on me. But Cindy did.

It happened on the Sunday of the "party." Jack and Cindy Frazer and myself were the only ones lounging around their luxurious living room having cocktails and snacking on hors d'oeuvres Cindy whipped up and listening to Dave Brubeck tapes. Jack and Cindy were seated on a huge Mediterranean divan facing me. And as the liquor fuzzied my brain a bit I felt less inclined to stop enjoying the sight of Cindy's legs. She was seated properly, hem of her dress draped just above her dimpled knees, one gorgeous leg folded over the other. But when she first sat down I caught a glimpse of her thighs and I sat there waiting for the moment she'd uncross and cross her legs again.

"Well," said Jack, interrupting my favorite pastime, "what shall we do until the others arrive?"

What did he mean "do?" I just wanted to stay put. "Oh, I'm content. Thank you." I sipped on my drink, absorbing the music, and waited for an opening to lay out a scheme in my mind. A phone rang. Jack graciously excused himself. "Pardon me for a moment, Irwin," he said. "Probably someone calling to say they can't make it. Cindy'll keep you entertained." With that Jack was out of the room. And I resumed gazing at Cindy's legs.

"Will you be staying over in Dallas long, Irwin?" asked Cindy, remaining charming and composed.

Maybe. I thought, with just the right weight of words I could lead her to believe I was looking for a location for another B. Altman store. Then, not say anything more about it. She could tell her husband about it after I leave. "Just long enough to find a location," I said. Then shifting the subject so she couldn't pry further, I said, "Did you decorate this room yourself—it's really relaxing."

"Thank you. Yes. Well, with a little help from Jack." She was obviously taken in, and she glowed.

"Can I fix you another drink?"

I was going to refuse. But then I figured, what the hell, this is enjoyable—and I have time to work out my scheme. Just set it aside. Take a day off. Relax. "Thank you. I would appreciate another."

She got up and walked over to get my glass as Jack returned from the other room, saying, "I am terribly sorry—problems in one of our stores. (We're open Sundays you know.) And it's a sticky one. It'll require the attention of upper management. Not my department, but ol' Les isn't around. So, I'm it. Anyway, Irwin, I want you to stay. The others should be arriving any minute. I'll see you again?"

"Oh, sure," I said. "Maybe, tonight, when you get back."

"Don't count on it. May have to go to the office after I check things at the store," he said apologetically. Then he kissed Cindy. "Don't wait up, love. Tell everyone hello for me—and be nice to Irwin. Show him around the house. Maybe he'll want to buy it." Then he was gone.

"Now. Let me get you that drink." Cindy said. "Jack's been wanting to put the bar in here. But I won't let him. I like it better where it is. Come—I'll show you . . . I don't think anyone will show up this late. And if they do, I won't answer the door. Okay with you?" she said, as if she knew it would be. And it was—it was. "We call this our guest room," said Cindy as we entered an enormous bedroom furnished in massive Mediterranean. Then pointing to a sliding mirrored wall she said, "Sauna and showers in there. Shall we?"

"I heard you say 'we.' But what about Jack—won't he . . .?"

"He'd only join us if he did happen to come back this quickly. Anyway, he won't. Let me get you a robe. Nothing like showers and sauna to make a person feel renewed."

Cindy reached into a closet and brought out a blue terry-cloth robe. "This should work fine, Irwin," she said handing me the robe, "Now I'll fix that drink. Same thing? let's see, that was a vodka martini—straight up, wasn't it . . . or can I fix something very special for you."

"Special?"

"Yes. Secret concoction. Can't ask what it is."

"I'll try anything once," I said. "Mind if I throw the robe on the bed?"

"Please do," she smiled. "Why don't you change while I fix your drink—won't take long." She walked over to the bar and busied herself while keeping up a light, social chatter. The kind of talk that doesn't require response. I couldn't take my eyes away from her, every motion smooth, sensual, perfect. It didn't bother me that Jack may have decided to turn around and come back home. I believed Cindy when she said that he'd "join us." Would I have joined them if he had decided that three's not a crowd? Don't know. But something told me that he wouldn't return—not just then. And I intuitively felt that there were more important things on Jack's mind than worrying about Cindy. He'd already made it clear to me that he was "expanded" in his thinking.

For a moment at the church social I thought Jack meant that he and Cindy considered themselves spiritually expanded. But I changed my mind the moment he said "our Cindy." And I knew upon that statement that Jack had intended that he'd play sultan and that I would be the prince visiting from afar. Though I admit that I thought it would be one of their "expanded" friends I'd be introduced to for an evening's relaxation, not Cindy. I did have vivid pictures of spouse-swapping going on—and I'd heard that in some circles, swap parties were considered the "expanded" way of life, but when Jack mentioned something about my "buying it"—the house, there was no further speculation on my part. Cindy was the inducement for whatever the Frazers had in mind. They thought they had a "live one" on their hands. And far be it from me to spoil the illusion. Not when the inducement came in a gorgeous package named Cindy.

So, I decided to play naive—a game I'd learned almost twenty years before in San Diego. What the hell . . . if Jack Frazer couldn't lead me to his employer's coffers, I'd have fun finding my way to another source.

"Still haven't changed, Irwin?" Cindy asked as though she hadn't had her eyes on me all the while she fixed our drinks.

"No. Waiting to have a drink with you first."

She handed my drink to me. "Of course. But, if you don't mind, I'd like to change." Pointing to an overstuffed velvet-covered chair she said, "Have a seat. No need to stand. Taste your drink. Tell me if you like it."

I did as she asked. The drink tasted like a souped-up collins. "Different. What do you call it?"

"Aphrodite," she said.

"Aphrodite, huh?" I replied, tasting the concoction once

more. "Well, certainly more romantic than Bloody Mary."

"I agree," she said. "And it brings about everything it's name implies. So, if you aren't in the mood for an evening of magic, better say so—ever experimented with magic? Jack and I do."

"Oh, when I was a child I used to. Had an aunt. Eccentric. Believed in magic. Teleportation and so forth. She used to promise me that someday she would take me to a planet called Lam," I said, making light of it. But at that moment my mind did transport me back to Mitzi's apartment and the hours we'd spent in her bed. "And as I became older, I involved myself in cabalistic studies—tree of life and so forth—and the Altman family is Jewish, so I was practically weaned on Hebrew mysticism. But, the world of business keeps me away from studying, these days. That's why I enjoy, whatever chance I get, to go to Science of Mind churches—spiritualist churches too—just depending on my mood."

"Interesting," Cindy said. "We should talk about it more. But I'm serious about the effects of your drink. You should, after one Aphrodite, become most uninhibited."

Then, handing me her glass she said, "Clothes are a containment. Would you mind if I undressed. Or if you prefer, you can undress me. Which shall it be?"

I'd been in similar situations, and Cindy's directness was not unique. No. Not at all. What was unique was her sudden request to be naked and I wasn't ready to deal with it. I'd planned a slow buildup. The tone of her directness made it clear that she didn't mind if I kept my clothes on—for a while—but that she herself had no intentions of staying dressed. And now she was standing directly in front of me.

What was it Aunt Mitzi had said? That I could, if I wanted to, lift her skirt and look at her to my heart's content. I could do so. And I did. And I recalled the exciting voyage—no longer childhood's game—into the mysterious, sometimes torrential, sometimes calm, deep, dark waters of her being. "Here, darling—that's it . . . gently now . . . be gentle . . .

always gentle . . . at least to begin with . . . wait for the storm before you hold on so tightly. . . ."

So many years had passed since that day. And I had succeeded, until Cindy came along, in pushing the memory of Mitzi out of my consciousness. I'd even adopted a "so what" attitude regarding the two years spent under Mitzi's sexual direction. I liked it. Enjoyed it. And even after my realization of the taboo involved and my knowing that I would never again become sexually involved with her, or any blood relative for that matter, I could never deny the fact that I liked sex with Mitzi. Could never deny the fact that I loved Mitzi. Love in a childlike way, perhaps. Sick? Perhaps. Sick by society's measure for certain. And I had become aware of the fact that there were children who were unwilling, innocent victims of child molesters. But, I was not unwilling. And until I met Sylvia, my first wife, I missed Mitzi just as much as anyone who found themselves separated from a loved one. She was my first love.

During the days I knew Cindy and Jack my main priority was to find the way to the big score. Anything else was a bonus. And that's exactly what Cindy was to me. A bonus. And I recall that I wanted very much to undress her.

"Aphrodite lives," I said, and I placed the cocktail glasses on the floor beside my chair. Cindy didn't move. She just kept her stance in front of me, waiting for my answer. I placed a hand on her stomach and said, "I must admit, I find you fascinating."

"I know. I noticed your gaze in the living room." She stepped back a little and my hands fell to my lap. "You can do anything with me you desire," she said gently, "but there's only three rules."

"What are they?"

"First, you must understand completely that magic is an integral part of my life; second, while whatever we do will be expressed in physical joys, the vibrations, energy, must be directed to a definite purpose; and third, no violence of any kind."

Now, I had created trips like that myself. And Cindy was beginning to sound like my female counterpart. I looked around the room to see if there was a crystal ball or incense receptacle I might have missed. But there were none. Not even a deck of cards or I Ching sticks. None of the trappings I'd been accustomed to. "I agree, Cindy. After all, I too am a lifelong student of the arts."

"Jack is also—just that—a student. He is learning. Though at times he loses sight of the fact that all of this—our material belongings—is a direct result of magic."

Knowing that I never had a nickel I didn't steal or work for, and knowing that Jack had a hell of an income, because of his position, and having met and cultivated a few magic nuts myself, I wondered if Cindy believed her own bullshit. She sure as hell seemed sincere. After years of pursuing the occult, I'd come to the conclusion that even if there were "truths" to be found, its application to the world in which we live was next to impossible; and the only thing that kept me from telling her was the fact that I wanted to screw her. So what if it was on her terms.

"Did you ever wonder why you always seem to gravitate to people who practice magic?" she asked.

"Well, mysticism has been a part of my life—always. And I just naturally frequent places I would expect to find such people."

And when I said "naturally frequent such places," an enlightening wave of fear filled me. What if the cops had figured out that I frequent spiritualist churches, mind- expanding churches, or pursue the occult? Surely a couple of the women I'd "married" would have said something when they filed bigamy complaints. Then I remembered my first arrest had been accomplished by a lady cop. And I began to wonder if Cindy and Jack were cops.

Cindy noticed my preoccupation. "Irwin, what's the problem. Are you alright?"

"Oh, sure," I lied. "Just nerves. Like I said back at the church. Business pressures—that's all." I reached for my drink, drank it down, "I'm ready for that shower and sauna." I told myself that if Cindy were indeed a cop, she wouldn't get naked. She was still dressed, and I was about to find out if she'd stepped away from my hands for reasons other than talk.

"Of course," she said, "I'm glad you drank Aphrodite down. Now will you undress me—or shall I . . ." She stepped forward again. I leaned forward and lifted her dress up just above her hips. She was wearing purple bikini panties, an exciting contrast to her smooth, pale belly. I pulled her close and kissed her navel, put her dress down in place, stood up and took her in my arms.

"Irwin," she whispered, "Remember, I said there had to be a definite purpose. The energy, Irwin—don't let it go to waste. Want something besides my body. Want something. . .."

I did want something besides her body. I wanted a last score. The big one. The liquor had begun to lull me. And I remember saying, "I do. Lots of money."

"More than the Altman store fortune?"

"Yes, lots more."

"Good. Then do with me what you will, but let's shower first. Let's start in the shower—please." Then, she undressed me. Stroked and kissed my "core of energy," she called it. "Now let's shower." She fixed more Aphrodite. Then I followed her through the mirrored doors thinking of Alice in Wonderland. Showering with Cindy was a ritual of fragrant steaming suds that we massaged gently all over each other's bodies, rinsed away, repeated, several times. Between hot and cold rinsings and stimulating sudsings we drank more of Cindy's Aphrodite. "Think of me as a channel into which you can pour energy, Irwin. Think of this before we close the circuit." My head was spinning. And I recalled how Mitzi and I played button, button. My thoughts vacillated between Mitzi and wondering if lady cops did give blow jobs to their suspects—just to get them to open up more. Well, I recall thinking that if Cindy was a cop and she was trying to get a confession out of me it sure beat blanket parties and billy clubs. Well, I won't let her know that I suspect her. Get the full treatment. We rinsed, and Cindy turned the shower off.

"We won't dry. Just go into the sauna—next room."

"I don't know what's in those Aphrodites—but I feel tremendous," I said.

"I have a feeling I may wind up telling you what's in them. But not right now. I want you to concentrate on your field of energy."

Everything about Cindy was perfect. And to make it even more perfect for me was her tiny titties. And I kissed them. "And what about you, Cindy. What do you want?"

"I'll tell you later. Not now. Don't break the thought of what you are after."

After a few minutes in the sauna and final rinse in the shower, we went back to the bedroom. And I recall thinking in my liquored-up state of mind, looking around at all that luxury, if maybe Cindy did indeed have magic powers. As we got into bed, I said, "If you are a sorceress, you're the first real one I've met in years."

"Shh. Not now. Lay still. Let me please you. Think of all the money in the world."

She kissed every inch of my body, and I felt fuzzy. I began to respond and then I found my goal. My head below her belly I said, "Cindy, I want to drink you. I want you inside of me."

"But, I am already—a little." And I knew she was referring to the Aphrodite.

"I want more . . . now . . . from you . . . not from a mixture.I want your magic now. I've tried everything . . . nothing works. Nothing. Wet me, Cindy, let me drink you . . . Mitzi. . . ."

"Is Mitzi who you want me to be? Is that why you called me Mitzi?" Cindy's voice was filled with compassion. "Tell me, Irwin, tell me, please, I've got to know what you want."

"Yes, my God, yes, I want my life back!"

And I was bathed. I fell asleep.

With morning came confusion. I woke. Cindy was nowhere in sight. So, I laid in bed for a while trying to put the pieces of the night before together. But nothing made much sense. Though, I knew I'd be let in on the whole secret soon. I freshened up with a shower, dressed, went into the living room where I was greeted by Jack Frazer. "Morning. Sleep okay?" he said pleasantly. And his face was totally noncommittal.

"Oh yes. Yes, thank you." This Jack Frazer was a puzzle.

"Cindy sends her apologies but she had an appointment and didn't want to wake you. In fact I'm due at the office soon. But I've got something to discuss with you. Do you mind?"

"No. Not at all." Now it was coming. I'd find out.

"Like some coffee?" he said.

"No. No thanks." I just wanted to get on with it. The night before had been different. I felt good. Even considered a repeat if I could get it.

"I'll be direct. You're a person, obviously, of some financial depth. And I'm in some difficulty. A whole lot of difficulty. And as long as you're going to open a store here—how would you like to buy my home?"

Well, at least my front had worked; Jack and Cindy obviously thought I was Mister Money. "Why don't you put it up for sale in the ordinary way?"

"I need more than the house is worth."

"Honesty is refreshing. But I don't understand why you think I'd be willing to pay more than it's worth. Not unless you have hidden cameras around here and are thinking of selling me some pictures of last night's action to go with the house."

I couldn't believe what followed. Jack was actually offended at my insinuation. Not defensive at all. Simply offended. "Well, I can see that my snap judgment yesterday was stupid. So, why don't we just forget it."

I wasn't willing to forget it. Not just then. I wanted more of Cindy. "Sorry, no offense meant. It's just that some years ago (you know how vulnerable an Altman can be) someone did try to blackmail me. Had to report him to the law. Dirty affair." Hell, that was about the most ridiculous story I could think of. Me. Calling the law . . . I wouldn't have at that time called the law for any reason. Not and take a chance of being uncovered myself. Hell, no. But the story was part of my stock-in-trade. All honest folk talk about calling the cops, even on their neighbors. And I wanted an honest-folk image.

Anyway, Jack intrigued me. And I wanted to hear more. "Okay," he said. "I'll spell it out for you. Do you agree that Cindy is special?"

"Yes, very much so."

"Her life is completely devoted to her beliefs and keeping her men physically and mentally free of garbage. But only the very rich can afford the luxury of Cindy. And we decided that as soon as someone came along that we felt could take over we'd . . . I'd sell out."

"I see." I didn't not really. But I figured that Cindy had him talked into that idea. He was probably busting his balls trying to keep it together.

"The house is mortgaged up to the limit—so even if we got a divorce she wouldn't be getting anything. We've been looking around for a new man for Cindy, or at least someone that had enough money to play with. See, Cindy goes with the house."

I couldn't help but wonder what school of drama Cindy attended. She was good. This guy's brains were really mushy.

In my prison cell, as I became aware of my own garbage, I realized I felt sorry for him. And Cindy was my female counterpart—just as I had thought. But what a fantastic self-image that girl had. What a fantastic playmate for a politician she'd make—as long as the money flowed, she'd extract the garbage from his soul. And when he felt low enough for his life of fucking people around, Cindy could pee all over him. And make it better—for a while.

Jack was desperate. And I took advantage. I'd talked him into letting me have the house and Cindy for a few weeks, "just to give me a chance to get my other business out of the way. Then we might make a transaction. I'll even make a month's mortgage payment. And I'll let you stay in my apartment." He was whipped, had no choice. And I must have needed the treatment Cindy had to offer, because I was willing to let go of almost all the money I'd saved to invest in my score to pay for it. Only I thought I was paying for a few kicks, and another place to hide. And if I had enough change to put in the slot in the woman-machine I could have stayed buried in gumballs till they cover me over with earth.

The fact that I'd called out in the night for Mitzi nagged at me a bit. But it didn't tear me apart as much as one night while drowning in Cindy's fantasy world, I cried for my fatherless children. "Cry, Irwin, cry," said Cindy. "Empty yourself of tears." And when I let go of the last fragment of fantasies of Cindy, I wondered vaguely how I could save the last falling tear, and if it fell, who would shed a tear for its passing: the prison guards—the bulls? No. They'd bury me standing up. My wives? They'd pee on my grave. My children? They don't even know me. Myself? I don't even know myself. My mother? Would she bury me with father's ruby ring but keep his gold lapel-watch just for old time's sake?

XI

Before I went to Folsom Prison, a police investigator told me that one of my wives, Jennifer, the one from Denver (I think), told him in anger, "That son-of-a-bitchin' Irwin should register his mouth—like a boxer, his mouth is a *lethal weapon!*" Yes. Jennifer would be likely to have said to the police inspector that my mouth was a "lethal weapon." In bed, she had a multitude of flattering descriptions for my mouth—so why not "lethal weapon."

Jennifer and I met in the fall of nineteen-seventy on a plane from Dallas, Texas, to Denver, Colorado. I was so pissed that day bcause a caper I had such high hopes for had gone flat, that I didn't pay attention to the fact that I was seated next to a lovely, long-legged redhead. Well, shit, I was damned near broke. I had thrown a sizeable amount of money into that caper in Dallas—money I'd earned legitimately, selling advertising. I'd sacrificed by living in cheap hotel rooms and eating in skid row restaurants and not spending a nickel for entertainment—hell, I even went without pussy. Because, I'd decided after twenty years of scheming, that I was going to make the one big score and retire from crime. Up to that episode, except on two occasions, I'd stolen only enough money to support my "traveling-first-class" lifestyle, mingling with and screwing fancy and some not-so-fancy women after an evening of theater, ballet, or a session at a seance where I'd hoped to make contact with Zayda. Also, I bought books—metaphysics, black magic, witchcraft—all of which I'd leave behind with the ladies—some of whom thought they were married to an heir to a department store fortune, a mystic who could put them in a trance and guide them through their past lives, or (my favorite image) the nephew of a wealthy eccentric aunt who "thought she owned me . . . just because she has me on an allowance . . . expects me to escort her halfway around the world while she collects *objets trouvé* or young lovers . . . after all, I do have a life of my own!"

But none of the women knew that I had a legal wife.

But I was becoming lonely. And I had met some warm, loving, sensitive, intelligent and generous people, who I would have wanted, under different circumstances, for friends. People who thought they had a friend in me. But I always wound up duping and disappointing them.

I'd always felt badly about ripping people off emotionally. And, I always became concerned about the bankers and tellers I'd tricked into exchanging the bank's money for worthless paper. But around nineteen-seventy my conscience began actually to pain me, and cause me sleeplessness and I thought everyone who met me knew I was a crook.

Why, then, didn't I stop right there? Well, I'd already heard of one warrant out on me that was certain to get me a ride to prison, and I didn't want to go to prison. And I wasn't certain just how many of my wives were looking for me. So, I thought: One good score. A final change of identity, and a happy life. Somewhere. Maybe. By then I'd had so many different identities I'd almost forgotten who I was. Maybe that's why I decided, in Dallas, to use my own name.

In any event this would be the Big One. I even pictured myself sticking a huge sum of money in a box and mailing it to Theresa. For her and our daughter. Much of my feelings of guilt were wrapped up in Theresa and our kid. In nineteen-sixty-eight I had gone home for a while. Theresa and I had agreed to try to make a go of it. But I stayed around only long enough to get a patent on a hair roller I invented, and I was off to New York to try to sell it.

I couldn't get Theresa and my daughter, Terri, out of my thoughts. And they were woven into my other depressive thoughts on that plane to Denver. So it wasn't until the stewardess asked me if I'd like a drink and I said, "Yes, a CC and water please," that I'd taken real notice of Jennifer. She ordered a coke—and I didn't speak to her until the stewardess brought the drinks back.

"Going to Denver?" I asked, smiling.

"Yeah, that's home. Be glad to get there. You too?"

"Uh-huh—but San Francisco's home." I said while trying to formulate a plausible story in my mind. A story that would get me into her bed.

"Oh, a traveling salesman?"

"No. Actually, I'm in research. And I'm going to Denver to visit a group of people who are into similar work." That was true enough. I'd heard there was a coven of witches in Denver. And I did want to locate them.

"Oh. What area of research are you in?"

Here was my chance. "Parapsychology. And right now I'm doing a study on reincarnation—past lives and so forth. And I've recently discovered a way to determine how many past lives a person has had by studying the lines on the palms of their hands . . . Doing a paper on it."

"Oh. You mean like palm reading? Fortune-telling?"

"Not exactly fortune-telling. But there is a way of determining destiny."

"Fascinating. I wish I'd known you before I got my divorce."

"Oh. Sorry. Divorce can be painful."

"Well. It was coming. My fault really. But here we are, strangers, I shouldn't unload on you. Sorry. How long will you be in Denver?"

"Oh, about a week, if all goes well—may I call you?"

"Do! By all means. Here, I'll give you my phone number," she smiled, and opened her purse and reached in for her billfold. Unfastening it she withdrew a business card. Handing it to me she explained, "Not in real estate anymore—but the number's the same." I took the card, and watched her fasten her billfold. I made silent note of a neat row of credit cards.

"I'll be staying at the Hilton. The name is Richards—Bart Richards. And I will call you," I said. Then, looking at the card she gave me, "Jennifer, lovely. I like it."

"Thanks, Bart," she said, raising her glass in a toast. "I think we'll be friends."

. . . "Hello, Jennifer?"

"Yes. Who's calling? Your voice doesn't sound familiar."

"Bart Richards—the fellow you met on the plane." I didn't have any I.D. for the "Bart Richards" name I plucked out of the air on the plane that day, but I figured I could take care of that if necessary.

"Oh, Bart—the psychic. How are you? I tried to reach you at the Hilton, but I guess you decided not to stay there."

"Yeah. Didn't feel like staying downtown." That was true. Too many cops in the downtown area. And the Hilton was more money than I could afford. In fact, a few more days and I'd probably be looking for a bunk in the Salvation Army or a rescue mission. But I found a job on Thursday selling circus tickets on the phone, and I was to start work on Monday and I wasn't certain if I could make my cash stretch, remembered Jennifer and those credit cards I saw sticking out of her billfold, and decided to call her.

"Where are you staying?"

"At the Motel Flamingo."

"Oh, that's not far from where I live. Listen, I'm having a few friends over this Saturday. Nothing formal—and I know they'd be fascinated to meet a psychic."

"Saturday." Too far away I thought. "Sounds great. Be happy to. Listen, I know this is short notice for someone who must have their phone ringing off the wall every minute but how about a drink tonight?"

"No, the phone stays pretty quiet these days—just my ex-husband, when he's drinking too much. But tonight I was going to wash my hair—I'm a mess."

"You? a mess. Impossible. But I don't want to foul up your schedule—so, we'll make it another time." I'd learned that by not pressing a woman was a quick way to get her to say, "Yes." And I hoped Jennifer was like all the others.

"You know, I could use a drink. Have a car yet?"

"No. I'm going to rent one next week."

"What time can I pick you up?" she said.

Not wanting to get stuck for dinner I said, "How about eight. I have an appointment at six, but I know I'll be back by eight o'clock."

"Eight's okay. There'a a cocktail lounge at the Flamingo, isn't there?"

"Uh-huh."

"See you there at eight. Bye."

"See you." I hung up the phone, reached in my pocket, felt my money. No need to count it. I had exactly twenty-seven dollars and some change. So, whatever I did to cure my lousy financial condition would have to be done quickly. Only, I recall, I hoped I wouldn't have to resort to Jennifer's credit cards.

Jennifer showed up at the Flamingo Fireside Lounge promptly at eight, and we took a table close to the fireplace. Ordered whiskey sours and it was Jennifer that led our conversation. "Your work sounds interesting, Bart. Do you get into astrology much?"

"No. Not really. I'm more interested in past-life research."

"Oh, that's right you did say so on the plane. Something to do with handprints. Do you really believe people reincarnate?"

"Well, my grandfather believed it. And I suppose I follow in his footsteps. I'm glad you said, 'believe' because Zayda—Grandfather—always said, 'To believe is not to know for sure; you gotta keep wondering, when you don't know something for sure.'"

"Oh, he must have been an interesting man. Sounds different, anyway. I never knew my grandparents. You're fortunate."

Fortunate? A fleeting picture of a child sitting on a platform swing crossed my mind. But talking with Jennifer I didn't stop to consider fortune or dwell in the gardens of childhood. My only consideration was survival until I got on the phone promoting circus tickets the following Monday. "Yeah. Zayda was a good man." I said reflectively. "And I guess I've made a few discoveries regarding past lives, but my research seems to take me from one path to the other. I hear a story, and track it down. Like the one about the eight-year- old girl in Italy who kept nagging her parents to take her to a village five hundred miles from their own—a village she'd never seen. Finally, in order to stop her nagging, her parents pack up and take her there. Upon arrival the little girl directs them to a small house at the far edge of the village, a house she'd described in detail even before she laid eyes on it. So, there they are—knocking on the door of a stranger's house. A guy opens the door and this little eight-year-old girl calls him by name and asks him how the children are doing—calls all the children by name too. Then, she suddenly recalls that this guy standing in the doorway was her husband before she died. 'When did your wife die,' he was asked by researchers and reporters. So he produces a death certificate that says she passed on eight years ago on the day of that eight-year-old girl's birth."

"Yes, it seems I remember reading something about that. Unnerving, isn't it?" Jennifer's mood changed. She'd been gay and social and even warm. "You know, Bart, if there is another life I'd wish to be a little happier. That's all. Just a little."

"Beautiful woman like you? C'mon, you couldn't be that unhappy. People get divorces every day. Miss him?"

"In a way. But it's not his fault. Really. Tell me, do you think I could find something out about my past life—if I had one at all?"

Now I had the opening I'd hoped for. "Certainly. But cocktail lounges are not conducive to psychic research, so it'll have to keep."

"What's involved? How do you go about it, getting into other lives?"

"Everyone has different methods. I study palm prints—left

and right—then I work through hypnosis."

"Hypnosis! Oh, that's marvelous. I've been wanting to go to a hypnotist for the longest time—just haven't gotten around to it. Say, if it's not imposing would you like to come out to my house and have some coffee? I'll take you back to the motel later, but I sure want to talk to you—and like you said, cocktail lounges are not conducive to anything personal. I do have a problem."

Her emphasis on "anything personal" was the signal. "Yes, I'd be happy to."

We drove out to Jennifer's house and once we were seated on the sofa with our coffees Jennifer said, "I'm not the kind of person to waste time, so I have a direct question for you."

"Sure."

"Can you really hypnotize people?"

"Yes. Of course there's some simple tests to see if you're susceptible."

"Tests?"

"Simple tests. And then you must want something from the experience."

"You won't do anything to make me look foolish—will you?"

"No. But it could be that hypnosis is not the way to solve your problem or find out about your past lives."

"I'm more interested in my immediate problem. I've been to doctors and they're not able to find the cause of my problem. And I'm thirty years old. If I don't get to it now, I don't know if I ever will."

"Some kind of pain you can't locate the cause of—that's common," I said.

"No. You might say it's . . . well, what's the difference . . . we're not children . . . I can't make it . . . can't have an orgasm . . . at least not anything like I hear about."

For a moment I thought Jennifer was looking for an excuse to go to bed with me, but I thought differently when I recalled she'd said that her divorce was not her husband's fault. And even if it was a game she'd made up—it would still serve my original purpose. "There are women who go through their life without an orgasm. They seem to adjust."

"Well, this is one woman that's made up her mind to do something about it. I lost a good husband—two husbands (to be perfectly honest), they both got worn down, disgusted, frustrated and concerned about their own sexuality in the process of trying to bring me about. Now, I'm an intelligent person, and I like being close to someone who appeals to me—but I'm getting to a point where I'll put a zipper on it and forget the whole thing."

It wasn't until Jennifer became conversantly intimate that I told myself she could be a cop. Everyone, lately, had become suspect to me. I'd even expected Cindy in Dallas to get out of bed and pull a badge on me. Then I remembered the new "kicks" I'd discovered with Cindy and decided that Jennifer's "problem" would be a good way to satisfy my new sexual games and maybe help her at the same time. And if Jennifer did turn out to be a cop it would just mean my time had come.

"Have you ever really cut loose of all inhibitions?" I asked Jennifer.

"If you mean do I go for anything in bed, the answer's yes. I don't think I'm inhibited."

"You said "in bed." Does that mean "in bed" is the only place?"

Jennifer didn't embarrass. "No. All over the house. Doesn't matter."

"Stand up and raise your dress." I commanded gently.

"Huh?" She was stunned. "You mean right now?"

"Right now." I said, firmly. She stood up in front of me and raised her dress up. Embroidered giraffes were peeking around the inseam of her pink pants. With both hands I pulled her pants down until the last giraffe rolled out of sight. Then I reached around, pulled her close to me, and kissed her below her belly button.

"You don't waste time, either, do you," she said. Then she

fell across my lap. And all through the night I proceeded to see if I could help her. I couldn't, but she made it fun trying. And she didn't insult my masculinity. Jennifer was sincere.

The following morning I had my story together. "My name's not Bart Richards," I told her. "It's Altman. And I'm hiding from my family in New York. But I'm going to have to get in touch with my aunt—because I'm running out of spending money."

"Oh, one of those poor little rich boys, huh? I'll bet you have girl friends all over world."

"Ex-wives that keep me taking money from my aunt. But, next month there's a lump-sum settlement on my inheritance. Say, by the way, do you mind if I make a collect call from your phone—want to get a hold of my aunt before she decides to take a trip."

Experience taught me that women who were after money would be willing to make little investments of their own such as long distance calls—and if the story is strong enough—they'll let you move in. And with a little practice you can make a telephone call to nowhere and hold a conversation that sounds authentic. "Why don't you just dial direct, we can pay the bill when it comes." Jennifer offered.

She tipped herself off when she said "dial direct" and "we can pay the bill." She'd taken possession of her "poor little rich boy."

So, I dialed the time in New York and held the receiver tight to my ear. That way the recording on the other end wouldn't leak out. "Hello, Auntie, how are you?"

"The time is ten-fifty-five and twenty seconds."

"Oh, the old hay fever acting up, huh? I won't keep you long. What's that?"

"The time is ten-fifty-five and thirty seconds . . . The time is ten-fifty-five and forty seconds . . . the time is ten-fifty-five and fifty seconds . . . the time is ten-fifty-six . . ."

"Fifty-sixth birthday. No, I haven't forgotten. I'll send a card and some roses. Listen, Auntie dear, I've really let myself run short—very short this time—so if you can send a few thousand I'd appreciate it."

" . . . and thirty seconds. . . ."

"Where to send it?" keeping the phone tightly to my ear and talking over the mouthpiece to Jennifer who was standing dreamily nearby, I said, "Jennifer, what's the address here?" She whispered.

"Forty-eight-ninety-two West Harvard." And I repeated the address into the phone.

" . . . No, Auntie, just a friend. No, Auntie, no one's after . . . do you have that address now? Repeat it to me."

" . . . is ten-fifty-ei . . . ."

"No, Auntie—not fifty-eight—forty-eight-ninety-two, West . . . Oh you've got that—good. When will you send it?"

" . . . the time is eleven o'clock . . ."

"Okay. Good talking to you. Bye." I hung up.

"Care for some coffee," Jennifer said trying to be nonchalant. But I could detect the excitement over her new find.

The night before Jennfier hadn't been willing to give me the Cindy treatment, but about an hour after I hung up on my mythical Auntie, not only did she fulfill my wish, she said, "You're right, Irwin, letting go works, I made it, I love you."

That was on a Friday. And I'd told Jennifer that Auntie would send the check out Monday—Tuesday the latest. " . . . and I do think we should be married, but would you believe I don't have a whole lot of cash on me. So we'll have to wait. I'll go on back to the motel and call you as soon as the money comes. Then we'll go to Reno and get married."

"You'll do no such thing. We'll drive out to your motel—pick up your things and you'll stay here with me."

"In fact. We'll go to my bank—get some money and fly to Reno tomorrow. Is that alright with you? I'll have to call my friends, tell them not to come over tomorrow. But we'll invite them when we get back."

Jennifer and I were married in Reno. And by the time we got back to Denver she wanted a divorce. "You should see a doctor—a good psychiatrist, Irwin. It's bad enough, the way you like your sex—maybe okay for some women, but not for me—but I had no idea you became so depressed and this business of thinking everyone is a private detective spying on you for your family is paranoid. Absurd."

"So, you go on back to the motel, and I'll call you when your check comes. I don't want any of your money—but if you can reimburse me for the trip to Reno I'd appreciate it. And you pay for the divorce."

When Jennifer sent me back to the motel I had a hundred dollars of her money. So, I called the circus ticket promoters, apologized for not showing up for work, and the manager said I could come to work the next day—Wednesday. Not even a week had passed since the night Jennifer and I had cocktails at the Flamingo Fireside Lounge.

One thing about phone promotions—you get paid daily. So I wasn't worried about surviving. But I was tremendously depressed. And I'd begun to wonder what my new "kicks" in sex meant and also how long it would take the law to catch up to me. Then, what would Jennifer think and do when she realized that there'd be no check from Auntie in her mailbox?

XII

I'd earned some decent money selling circus tickets and as always felt good when I could feel that soft green in my pocket. So when Sunday's sun woke me I felt in better spirits and I had better control of my imagination. Why not go to church? I asked myself. And, I went to a Science of Mind church on Colorado Boulevard. And it was there I met Diana and her son Craig.

There was the usual coffee social after services. Diana was having a coffee along with the other men and women chatting, exchanging good feelings and discussing esoteric sciences. I'd noticed Diana during the services. We'd exchanged smiles; not more than anyone else in church, but I'd decided our smiles were enough cause for me to start a conversation. It could have been her dark hair and green eyes that pulled me to her. It could even have been her slender, graceful figure. Or possibly the tasteful print dress she wore. Just the right splash of purple. Maybe it was the way she introduced me to her son Craig: "And this is my son. . . ." Her emphasis on "son" told me that she loved deeply the dark-haired lad who was no more than eleven years old. Maybe it was all those things and more.

"I'm Irwin, and I'm very happy to know you both." My solar plexus flipped. Craig went about gathering pamphlets to take with him, leaving Diana and I standing together. And gazing into her smiling green eyes, I felt a new experience. Suddenly, I wished, painfully, that I had never turned my back to reality. And just as painfully, I was aware that the law would catch up with me. I was determined to know Diana better, and for once I was at a loss for words. I tried to force conversation. It was awkward for both of us. "Have you read Emmet Fox?" I asked her, and I recall my insides shaking—just the way I shook that time with Aunt Mitzi.

"Oh, yes, I should say so. And others in that category. But I must admit I have a rough time with karma. And right now I'm mad at myself. I didn't stop to write a check this morning, and I don't think I've enough gas to get back home."

"I'm sorry. Can I help?" I wanted to help. No payback.

"No, thanks. But I appreciate the offer." Then she excused herself and mingled with the others. I walked to the pamphlet table and picked up a book, took five dollars from my pocket, stuck it in the book, then scribbled my telephone number and name on the inside of the cover. This was one woman whose feelings I wouldn't hurt. I walked up to her, excused myself for interrupting her conversation, handed her the book with the money tucked in it. "My phone number is inside."

"Oh, thanks. Maybe I'll call. Can't promise."

"That's okay—whatever." I turned and left. And I could not get her out of my thinking. And that evening, one of those few evenings I stayed in my room to read, the phone rang.

"Yes," I said.

A woman's voice said, "Irwin Altman?"

"Yes."

"Irwin Altman, for the good of God in you, I bless you and praise you. Thank you for the five dollars."

"Did you get home okay?"

"Yes. Thanks to you. I shouldn't have been so stupid. Where can I send the five?"

"Please don't send it at all. I may not be here long. It's okay—really. Listen, would you mind if I called sometime. Are you married?"

"I'd like to think about it before I give you my number. But, no, I'm not married. Are you?"

"Boy, am I married!" I laughed. "Remember the old woman who lived in a shoe?"

"Yes," she said and I could feel her smiling.

"Well, just change it around a bit. Start with 'There was an old man. . . .' "

"Let's see if I know what you mean," she sounded amused. " . . . who lived in a shoe, he had so many wives he didn't know what to do—why that's absurd. You're funny."

"Well, good for a laugh," I said and felt depressed.

"My phone number is nine-three-six-eight-three-o-one. But don't call before six—I work."

"What do you do, if I may ask?"

"I'm a psychiatric social worker. What about you?"

"I'm a thief."

"Funneee . . . Wives . . . a thief. You'd make a hell of a case for me. C'mon what do you do?"

Leaving well enough alone, not wanting to take further risk, I said, "I sell circus tickets."

"Oh, that sounds like fun. Travel?"

"Lots."

"I wish I could stay on the phone and talk some more, Irwin, but I'm going to a lecture with my niece. Will you call me?"

"Yes." I wasn't certain.

"Promise?"

"I promise. I'll call. Soon." Promise? It had been a long time since I made a promise—Mitzi made me keep a promise and broke my heart.

"Okay, then, I'll say 'bye for now." And the moment she hung up my solar plexus danced and I missed the sound of her voice. And I was torn between leaving Denver or staying around long enough to call her again. The phone rang again. It was Diana. "Irwin," she said, "the lecture is from eight to nine-fifteen—I should be home by ten—if you want to talk some more."

"Would you like me to come over instead?"

"Nope! Not tonight. Maybe not at all. But do call. Okay?"

It took a solid week of calling Diana before she gave me her consent to visit. And by that time I was in a state of frenzy.

Her home was modest, two-story frame, but expressed her marvelous mind by its walls of well-worn books, paintings, and tapestries—a depth I felt at our first meeting.

"Well," Diana said, "If it isn't the old man in the shoe. Come in. Welcome. And how do they say it in Hebrew—*Shalom.*"

"*Alechem-Shalom.*"

"Peace—how beautiful." Then, pointing to an overstuffed chair near an upright piano in the corner of her living room she said, "Sit and be at home." Sitting down I could see into part of the kitchen. A kitchen that had been well used for many years.

Diana sat on a couch to the right of the entrance to the kitchen. "So, now you see how I live. It's home. Raised my children here—by myself. Only Craig left at home now."

"Children. I have two—two girls."

"Still married?" she asked.

"Yes," I replied. Oh, there were the usual lies swimming around my head. But, I just couldn't lie to her. Maybe I was too busy trying to control the spasms in my solar plexus.

"Separated?"

"Long time. One child at home, Terri. Another I haven't seen for years, from my first marriage. First wife passed away."

"How long ago?" she asked.

And I had to think. Suddenly it dawned on me that it had been nineteen years since Sylvia's death. My God—where had it all gone? "Nineteen years ago. Long time. Very long. But say," I drew a deep breath, "You do sound like a social-worker. All those questions in five minutes' time." And I laughed so that she would know I was not offended. Just uncomfortable. She was a delight to behold. And I wanted her to know that she had freedom with me—but slowly.

"Sorry. Force of habit. Okay, let's talk about something else . . . want to speculate on life on other planets? I think there could be. Not like us maybe. But intelligent life forms—maybe even smarter than us—smarter. I said that to a friend of mine and I guess his ego went haywire at the thought of anyone smarter than he thinks he is. Besides, everything is alive and had its own intelligence, its own purpose for being, and every molecule, every atom strives to fulfill its purpose. Right?"

"Yes, we each have a purpose to fulfill, but we—human beings—choose our own purpose in life. There's a difference."

"Right," she said, "so we both have brains—now what do we do?"

"Where's your son?" I asked.

"Oh, he's upstairs. Think he's handsome? Say yes or leave."

"Yes."

"What else? Just yes . . . that's all?"

"Yes, you are lovely." I'd said nice things to women before. But saying this to Diana was painful. Because I felt as though I meant it. And I waited tensely for her reaction.

"Well, I can't say you're lovely, exactly—but for a start, you're nice, and I like you. You still have to pass the Craig test."

"How does that work?"

"If I scream for help, he'll come sliding down the banister and kick you out. If I call up gently, and ask him to come down and say hello to you it will make him know he's still a part of the day's cares."

"Why don't you call him—gently."

"Craig, come down and say hello to the old man in the shoe." We laughed. And as Craig descended the stairs, I knew I had a family to care about—but was it too late?

That night, after Craig went to sleep, I told Diana the whole story. It took until four A.M.

"You can't stay," Diana said. "But call me as soon as you get back to your room. I'll worry about you."

I kissed her. And left, wondering if she'd call the cops. And hoping that I didn't frighten her. And when I got back to my room, I called her. She'd waited up for my call. She liked me. Liked me for myself. Myself?

I'd forgotten about Cindy, forgotten about Jennifer—and a month passed. I worked, saw Diana and Craig, moved out of the motel, got an apartment—and fell in love. Deeply. It was a stormy affair. Diana went through hell trying to get me to purge myself of Mitzi. Trying to show me there was no cause for paranoia—at least in regard to our relationship.

Night after night we'd sit and talk. She went without sleep. She coped with my knocking on her bedroom window at three in the morning—once a week I'd do that. Just to be sure there wasn't another man in the house.

She'd greet me in hair rollers and give me coffee. "See? Wanna look in the closets? I'm not Mitzi. I think I'm the one who needs psychotherapy . . . Now go home, Irwin. Even if you never sleep, I do. Gotta keep my job—take care of my kid. Jealous that your momma wasn't that way. Maybe you kept her up all night too!" Then she'd smile and I'd go home.

"Irwin," she'd say, "the only way you're going to get well is to surrender to those warrants. Eventually they'll catch you. Maybe shoot you. Please, love, think about it. I'll still be around when you get out. I haven't married since my divorce, and don't intend to. Won't even marry you until Craig is grown. Marry you—with all those wives spread around. My Gawd. Get me a doctor. Quick."

I even put money together to pay Jennifer what I owed her. That took two years. And even though we were in the same city we never ran into each other. The night I paid Jennifer her money was the same night Diana phoned me. "Irwin. They were here!"

I knew only too well when Diana said "they" she meant cops. Still I wanted to hear the concrete reality from her own mouth. It had been a long time coming. And, on the other hand I recall hoping for the slim chance "they" could mean a more pleasant situation than the one I'd dreaded.

"Yes, Irwin, they—the law . . . here . . . asking about you." Diana said. She sounded distraught. "I said I'd known you but haven't seen you for a while, but I'm certain they didn't believe me. God! I'm glad I didn't let you move in with me. Not only because of Craig, but I don't think I could have coped well seeing you arrested. What will you do?"

Do? For the moment all I could think to do was to put the phone down and walk away. Fifteen years. I'd managed to keep a step ahead of the law. Ever since that ride I took to the nuthouse for the LaFamento caper I had avoided jail. So, I believed I could do it again. If the law buried me under fifteen years worth of swindles and six unhappy wives and laid me out for each count both federal and state, I'd have to live two hundred and ten years to pay society its due. Hell, it would take fifteen years just to transport me in chains from state to state for trials. Fifteen years of county jails. And the way laws change from moment to moment, by the time I'd reached the last state for prosecution an *under certain circumstances* death penalty for con men might be put to use. Might as well be dead.

And I'd gone, over those fifteen years, through episode after episode of wanting to be dead—but dead—the real dead, not the living death of jail or prison. Why? Well, ripping people off had always been for me a conflict of values. Solid values pumped into me by Zayda, and father's "roll of the dice" attitude. Further I'd developed a belief that the situation with Mitzi was entirely my doing. Especially because even after she told me it was wrong I still wanted to be with her. Hell, everyone knows that boys are snails and puppy-dog tails and girls are sugar and spice.

And not until Diana got hold of me did I begin to formulate different ideas. Even then, it was damned difficult for me to accept the fact that boys and girls alike could get their heads fucked up by sick adults—especially where the exquisite pleasure of sex is involved. And especially where Mitzi had given me the only "mother love" I'd ever known . . . the only female love in my childhood.

And I'd managed to keep Mitzi's "secret," protect Mitzi's image until I met Diana. In fact, I protected my whole family with images I created. Father's beatings became "concern and affection." Mother's brooding, bitterness, transforming me into her "nephew," became the marvelous Jewish Mama who totally devoted her life to her husband and son. Mitzi, became the niftiest aunt a kid could have. Zayda and Buba didn't need another image. And telling stories about them made my family package complete. And I am certain that the people I duped wondered how a person like myself who came from such a wonderful family could be so fucked up.

By the time Diana came into my life and said, "How come?" separating the facts from fantasies was like trying to paddle from the middle of a shapeless turbulent ocean to a shore completely out of my sight. I'd become powerless over my own bullshit. Her caring and coping and working with my insanity and paranoia, that included looking in her closets for hidden lovers, had at least begun to make me willing to take a tiny peek at my life.

Diana and Craig: hamburgers and drive-in movies, and trips to the petting-zoo and fixing busted pipes under the house, and spading the garden, and talking philosophy East and West, and discovering that all creation is "magic" with more wonders still to become manifest, *proper harmonious order.* "Hell, Irwin—or whatever your name is," Diana would say, "the most sophisticated space platforms ever built are the planets. . . ."

And because of Diana I was able to watch a child grow unmolested. "Soul mates?" She'd say referring to my thoughts about reincarnation and her close relationship with her son, Craig. "I don't know—how can you prove it? But tell me Irwin, how much more a mate of my 'soul' can anyone be than my own kid?"

Still, the day Diana called me to tell me the law was on my back I wasn't ready to surrender—even though those shores had now become visible over the horizon.

I stretched out on the bed, trying to figure a way out of town without being seen—nasty, frightening, vivid pictures screwed with my head. I'd imagine myself surrounded by squad cars: Red flashing lights, and brilliant spotlights flashing through the window of my room; demanding voices over loud speakers warning me, "Surrender! Come out or be shot out"; I could see myself fearfully stealing out the door, lights blinding me, my hands high in the air, "Don't shoot!" I scream at the shadows crouched behind the blinding lights, "I don't carry a gun!" Despite my pleas, I see a cop spring out from where he was crouched behind one of the black and white squad cars. He points a pistol at me. Shoots. I crumble. Dead.

As much as I needed to stop I couldn't chance surrendering to an asshole like the one I'd dreamed up. Sure. When I was a kid growing up in Zayda's house I broke some rules. Like one summer's day when I splattered Zayda's prize roses generously with white fence paint. For that creative act Zayda let me have it with a strap over my bare behind until my rump was raw and my cries turned into a whimpering, "Please stop." Then, he'd lay the strap down, draw me close to him, hug me, kiss me, and say firmly, "Sometimes, Irwin, justice is harsh. But remember, it should also be swift. And never punish for the same thing twice."

I've never forgotten my Zayda's words. And even as I ran just narrow inches from the law I remembered Zayda's strap. But, I reminded myself that bullets are not straps. And cops don't hug dead thieves. And justice is not swift. You can, if you don't make bail, rot in jail for a year waiting for trial.

When I was a kid, still sailing ice cream sticks, paper boats, and fallen maple tree leaves down gutter puddles, there was Officer Harris. He kept our neighborhood straight. Officer Harris was a huge man; he could escort two neighborhood drunks from the Italy Tavern to their homes on Beck Street, two blocks away, in one dragging sweep. No arguments. He'd even join in on a chorus of "My Wild Irish Rose," or "My Yiddisha Mama," on the way.

Officer Harris turned on the lights and gas for the orthodox Jewish families on the sabbath, and prayed to Jesus and the Holy Virgin Mary on Sunday. Officer Harris delivered babies. He stopped street fights, and broke up family spats that got out of hand. Officer Harris bought gigantic ice cream cones at Solomon's candy store on the corner of Beck and Longwood, for kids that helped old ladies across the street with their heavy shopping bags. We kids spent a hell of a lot of time just waiting on the corner for old ladies with shopping bags. And if Officer Harris wasn't around to pass out the reward we just kept track: so many ice cream cones for so many shopping bags. And we didn't cheat. "Cheat and sure you'll get my nightstick across your behinds. Everyone understand?" We understood.

And when Officer Harris rode up seated tall and somber on the saddle of a brown and white police horse to ride escort for neighborhood funerals, like when Buba died, we grew to understand that Officer Harris was a closely woven part of us. But we sure as shit didn't understand, when the news spread around the neighborhood that Officer Harris had caught a knife in the lungs while trying to break up a rumble at the Italy Tavern. He didn't call for help. And to my knowledge, Officer Harris never killed anyone. Officer Harris died. And the only medals he received were our tears of grief.

If Officer Harris were still alive in nineteen-seventy when the heat was laying heavy on my back I believe I'd have surrendered to him and figured out a way to make it look as though he'd busted me on his own steam. I'd have done that. Just for the sheer joy and pleasure it would have given me to see him get a medal, maybe a promotion, and perhaps a few "Ohs" and "Ahs." But Officer Harris was dead. And I no longer sailed paper boats, ice cream sticks, and maple tree leaves down gutter puddles. I no longer played Monopoly. And going to jail was no longer a shake, a spill, and a roll of the dice across a mythical world made up of colorful cardboard squares, miniature wood houses and slips of play money. For me, heading for jail had become a concrete fact. And unlike the days when the four freaks played Monopoly, when my time came to land in the real jail I damn sure wasn't going to pull my pants down to my shoes—not without a fight.

I wasn't going to jail. Not if I could help it. The jailer of the world would have to bring his jail to me. I hoped it'd be soon. Countless nights in countless motel rooms in countless cities I'd wear myself down to sleep praying, "Oh my God, please let them get me soon . . . or let me die in my sleep, don't want to wake up to another day . . . not in this life, or any other, if there is another life." *Another* life! Shit! Would it be like this? Or worse, maybe. Zayda said he believed there were other lives.

XIII

The law would get me eventually. That's just the way it would have to be. Eventually. I had no intention to stop, turn around, and walk into the cage. But I ached for rest. A place to stop. A place to be in peace. Even jail.

At times, when I think of jail I'm reminded of a game of Monopoly. When I was a kid we played chess, Lotto and so forth, but mostly we played Monopoly. My friends—Harvey the High I.Q., Philip the String Bean, and Frankie the Shrimp, (they called me Fatso)—we were the four P.S. 52 freaks—the oddballs none of the other kids would be seen with. And we were always together. We were inseparable. Any time you wanted to find any one of us all you had to do was go down to Zayda's wine cellar and there we'd be playing our favorite game, Monopoly: Go to jail! Go directly to jail! Do not pass go! Do not collect two hundred dollars! Whoever wound up on the jail square had to pull his pants and underwear down to his shoes and remain bare-assed until he got out of jail. But if we happened to be playing over at Harvey's fifth floor apartment on Longwood Avenue, where he lived with his mother, and, if his mother wasn't home, we'd open the window and take turns peeing out into the street. The idea being to see who could decorate the gutter with the widest water circles without hitting the maple trees, or dribbling on the window ledge. Harvey never played that game when he landed in jail. "I gotta practice on the piano," Harvey would whine. So, Frankie, Philip, and I would give Harvey a "free pass." Then, the three of us peed out the window while Harvey practiced "March Slav" or "Claire de Lune" on the piano. Well, it was a hell of a lot better than getting into street gang rumbles with some of the other kids.

One day we got tired of giving Harvey free passes so we ganged up on him and de-pantsed him. But we had made one mistake. We chose the wrong place: Zayda's wine cellar. We forgot to lock the door, and Aunt Mitzi caught us. There we were: marveling over Harvey's groin, laughing and being silly and being amazed at the huge size of his organ. After all we were twelve years old, and found anatomy fascinating. I was especially fascinated and also envious of my friends, because I was the only one who had not yet begun to sprout into puberty and I didn't get the same results from playing around as they did. Hell, I was still a soprano and their voices were beginning to change.

Aunt Mitzi just stood there, her hands on her hips, smiling broadly. She even seemed amused at seeing us: "You boys better go outside and play. If your grandfather catches you Irwin, it'll be the strap!"

I remember, she smiled at me. It was a different smile than usual. Not the same laughing smile of amusement she had when we stood one day watching the swinging monkeys at the zoo. Not the party smile that went with my birthday cake. And as she turned around to leave, it dawned on me that it was the same smile Mitzi lavished on my Uncle Dave, whenever he patted her on her marvelous rear.

Playing Monopoly or chess, or stinking up our homes with science experiments, or peeing out the fifth floor window at Harvey's apartment, or spending Saturday hanging around Solomon's corner candy store, or taking a trip on the subway to Manhattan to see a movie at the Roxy, or visiting the Museum of Natural History, or the planetarium, or taking the four-hour hike to the Bronx Park Zoo, was all on our same long list of exploring life. It didn't matter what we did as long as we did it together. We were sworn to a blood-brother oath. Our own club. Our own rules: no lies, no stealing, and try to get good grades in school so we could clean Mr. Levin's (our science teacher) boat some weekends. And "no girls, unless they wanna play doctor and not tell on us— but anyway, we can't allow girls in the club because they'd have a hard time weeweeing out the window," Frankie would argue. He always seemed to have a valid argument. He still does, even today. He has a criminal law practice in New York where he defends some of the kids who were getting into rumbles while we played Monopoly. But I know for a fact that one of the rumblers is a Supreme Court judge in New York. No way to figure how a person will grow.

"Our Lord God is good." Zayda would say, chanting as though he were in the synagogue, "because He made it so we have endless chances to feed and nourish our souls so that they'll grow rich with love, strong with patience, and tolerant. And tall and broad enough to embrace His total universe in every direction. . . ."

He didn't give me a chance to respond. But instead chanted on. "Someday, Irwin, you'll give a girl you love a rose. If it's real love one rose will do. And if it isn't real love then a whole garden filled with roses would say no more than a donkey pretending to be a butterfly, and have no more meaning than my friend Yankel who makes himself out to be a holy man, all the time blowing his big nose into the sacred shawl on the sabbath sundown just because he's too lazy to reach in his pocket for his handkerchief. And he may stay lazy until Sunday's sun shrouds his grave. And by then, Irwin, it's too late, maybe. And his soul, if the Creator wants it to, may come back dressed up like a big donkey. Then, Yankel would have to start learning all over again. Oy! Such horrible karma Yankel will have."

No. God damn it! I'm not going to jail. Maybe Zayda was right. If old man Yankel would indeed reincarnate as a donkey for just blowing his nose into the sacred shawl, then what would I be in the next life? Probably a poor piss ant destined to be stepped on by one of my ex-wives. Or maybe I'll come back as an amoeba in the water in the toilet of a ladies' restroom. Or maybe I'll come back as a woman—a bank teller. Now that would be poetic justice for a guy that bilks banks and preys upon the hearts of women. That's it! A female bank teller married to some slob. A drunk. An asshole who'll blacken my eyes and use my pussy for a warm hole to jack off into. Or maybe I'll be a young boy's aunt and I can teach him how to screw—like Aunt Mitzi taught me—I'd even let him cook Oriental food. Aunt Mitzi. What a loving human being. What would Mitzi be in the next life? My mother? No such luck. And what would mother be? Maybe, mother'll be a peacock.

Oh God damn! Let me extricate this fucked-up karma. Maybe the cop'll kill me. No! Be my kind of luck they don't aim straight. Cripple me for life. On purpose. God? Bullshit! God's a jack-off— a big prick pumping away over the planet Earth. But shit, man, God. There's got to be a fucking end to this. God of my grandfather, I want to love You again. Is it because I didn't feed the street singer that I am in hell or is it that I love Aunt Mitzi and do not honor my father and mother? There's got to be peace. Zayda stood half his life in front of the Torah in his stocking feet believing in Your peace.

I remember. He'd sit with me on the green platform swing in our garden and coach me over and over: "People should have peace of mind. Your wife is not a servant or a rug to be trampled on or a Hoover vacuum cleaner to suck up your *dreck*. No. Not your wife. Not your children. Not your friends. Not even a ragged beggar is a donkey born to pull your load. Because for the work of a donkey. God made a donkey. And now there's a truck to do the donkey's work. So, soon, maybe even the donkey may graze in peace.

"Peace?" I'd sigh. Then, just before another long night of tormenting half sleep, I'd ask myself aloud: Why, when I am aware of the magnitude of Zayda's God, why, then, do I blow my big nose like Yankel the donkey? Shit! No need to wait for another life, Zayda. The crap I plant pops open in the here and now. My constantly sterile sperm spits right back in my eye. Look, Zayda: see my garden? Over the whole United States. Endless rows of brilliantly colored carnivorous pussy plants. And they blossom morning, noon, and night. Every color under the sun. And over to your right are plush, green banks of stolen cash. Those dark blue clouds, Zayda? Oh, they are not clouds. Just a thick swarm of cops circling in on me. Who knows, maybe they'll land on the carnivorous pussy plants first. What's that you say, Zayda? Get a job and stop all this nonsense? Who'll give me job? I got my first red mark when I wound up in jail in Jackson, Mississippi, when I hitchhiked to New York to see you. I ran away from Mama. And the day I got out of jail you died.

What's that, Zayda? Am I blaming you? I'm sorry if it sounds that way—what shall I do, Zayda—what shall I do? . . . you're right, Zayda. You're right. I'll give myself up. I will.

From the barred windows of the "gray goose," the prison bus, I got my first glimpse of Folsom Prison. A gray stone monster, built in eighteen-ninety-five, it reminded me of the eerie house of terror I'd seen as a child in horror movies. We drove through the first gate and parked in front of the administration building, and filed out slowly so as not to trip over our chains. In the tiny administration building, we were unshackled, stripped, inspected for contraband such as guns, knives, and dope, then, we were handed a set of white coveralls, a bedding set that smelled of insecticide and a brown paper bag of toilet articles: razor, toothbrush, tooth powder, and a bar of soap.

There were thirty of us. And none of the men in the group had seen Folsom Prison before.

I surrendered in San Francisco because I wanted to see Theresa first. She had agreed to meet me at Jung's on Fifth and Market. "Just enough time for coffee, that's all," she had said on the phone, "you must realize, after all these years, I have my own life."

Theresa's "own life" must have agreed with her. I remember how lovely she looked as she walked over to my table and seated herself. "Remember how I drink my coffee?" she asked.

"Sure. Black. But aren't you going to say hello?"

"I'm not certain. I'm thinking that if I don't say hello I could pretend that we never said good-bye, and when I look in the mirror I won't see a single strand of white hair, or the memory of a single mistake."

"You look beautiful. Time has agreed with you."

"What about you, Irwin, has time been good?" Theresa asked sincerely.

I passed her question. "Theresa, the law wants me. I'm going to turn myself in. I wanted to see you first, thought maybe if there's time, I could see Terri . . . Theresa . . . my values . . . my life . . . wrong . . . completely wrong . . . saying I'm sorry doesn't change what has happened . . . but I want you to know that I am sorry—sorry for having hurt and embarrassed you, and for all the rip-offs I've made . . . Hell, I've even ripped myself off. There is nothing more to say about it. Words alone can't repair it, or make it right."

"For your own sake, I hope you mean what you say. As for as our own situation—you were not entirely to blame. I can be grossly disagreeable," she said, reaching for my hand. "But now is not the time for you to see Terri. Don't come back into her life until you can spend more time with her."

"I don't know what the courts will do with me. I'm expecting the worst. I'll try to stay in touch."

"Write to me. I'll answer. Maybe I'll visit. After all, we are still married, you know."

"Yeah, Honey, I know," and it was a comforting thought. And I found myself trying to pretend that we had never said good-bye as I climbed the steps leading into the Federal Building. I thought about turning back. And when I found myself face to face with two courteous F.B.I. agents, I was still thinking of turning back . . . but by then it was too late.

I found myself in a cell crowded with eleven other men in the San Francisco County Jail. Life seemed futile. I wanted to die. I found a double-edged blade on the writing table, walked to the rear of the cell, stepped into a shower stall, drew the curtain, and cut my wrists.

In handcuffs locked tight around my open cuts, in leg irons, two deputies stuffed me into a patrol car and drove me to the county hospital where an intern cleaned and dressed my wounds. "You'll need stitches. Want to see a psychiatrist?"

"No," I said, "I'll be O.K." I had nothing more to say. The intern stitched my wrists, gave me a tetanus shot, wished me "luck."

"Keep an eye on him," he told the deputies. "And here's a package of sleeping pills—give him one every night for a week."

Back at the jail they decided to stick me in a one-man cell. And every night for a week a deputy brought me a sleeping pill. I saved them up and one night I swallowed all of them. My body felt warm; I fell asleep.

I don't recall being carried out of the jail or being hauled back to the county hospital. I don't know how many days it took me to wake enough to realize I was handcuffed to a hospital bed. I do remember Dr. Bemus. He stood at the side of my bed, smiling, "You are now dead, and this is how you will spend eternity."

Out of the corner of my eye I scanned the ward. "Where's Nigger-Jesus?" I asked the doctor.

"Who?"

"Never mind . . . another lifetime."

"You mean you've been in a place like this before?"

"Uh-huh, long time ago."

"Why'd they ever let you out?"

"I don't know," I said sleepily, "something about it being too expensive to feed me . . . Fuck it, Doctor! Let me go to sleep!"

"Not yet. Someone wants to see you. Says she's your wife. Went to a lot of trouble to get permission from the good folks at the jail."

Dr. Bemus didn't wait for me to answer. He turned away saying, "I'll go out and send her in. Check on you tomorrow."

I watched him walk across the ward. An attendant who stood guard at the door let him out. In a few minutes Theresa entered, found her way to my bed, and stood where the doctor had been. She appeared to be angry. "I thought you were through running," she said.

"I thought so too. But I had forgotten how horrible jail could be. It's been a long time since I've been in the slammer. And when I realized that I could spend years locked up . . . death seems easier."

"For someone who believes in reincarnation, I'd say you're taking a big chance."

"How do you figure?"

"Well," Theresa said thoughtfully, "just supposing, mind you, that there is life after death, like you believe, and just supposing the law of karma in which you also claim to believe dictates that you pay your debts to the universe in full—in the flesh. That would mean, if I understand your thinking correctly, that you'll have to come back and go through the whole thing all over again. If that's the case, Irwin, do me a favor—if we do run into each other in another life, please forget you ever knew me." Tears filled Theresa's eyes. She turned and started to leave. "Do me another favor," she cried, turning toward me.

"What's that?"

"Live, Irwin, live!" She turned finally and left.

Doctor Bemus returned the following morning. "I'll give you a choice," he said. "You can go back to jail tomorrow and go through your court proceedings, or we can send you to an institution for the mentally ill until you feel well enough to go through the court process. Just keep in mind that there is no way to avoid the legal process."

I thought for a moment. Deciding that I did not want to delay the process any longer, I said, "Well, Doctor, I can't chance coming back like Yankel the donkey. Got to take care of my debts in the here and now."

I was returned to jail and the whole matter was treated as though it never happened. Finally, I pled guilty to numerous charges of fraud and I was ordered to prison.

XIV

My tiny cell on "Fish Row" was drab and dreary. "A reflection of myself," I thought. When I first set eyes on it, my first reaction was that they'd put me in a disciplinary cell. The hole. I used to hear the other prisoners around the county jail speak of it in grim, bitter tones. "They put me in the muthafucka for ninety days, once," one man in jail told me. "All I did, was take a piece of bread out of the mess hall. No visits. No mail. The whole time."

When I looked around the cage they stuck me in on my first day in Folsom Prison I thought they had made a mistake. Hell. I hadn't broken any rules. I figured when they realized the whole thing was a mistake they'd move me to a larger cell—one where the two bunks were not so close to the toilet. And maybe one where the toilet had a seat. After all, it's one thing to send a man to prison—take his freedom—but to stick him in a dungeon like this is outrageous. Look. I'm not denying I broke the law. I did. I swindled banks. And I didn't ask them to send me to a country club, or exile me to San Clemente. But neither did I expect a dungeon in a rat-infested castle of the vampires—which is the only literal description valid for Folsom Prison. There are no millionaires there. No. It is not a poorhouse. It is a house for the poor. The hopeless. The hardened criminal. Outraged as I was, I felt I belonged there. I hoped only for a slightly larger cell.

I told myself that they put me in the hole to show me how it was going to be if I stepped out of line. Sort of a preview. A way of letting a person know just who had the upper hand. And certainly when they realized they were dealing with a rational person they'd put me in the correct part of the prison.

I don't know how long I'd been brooding when a bull carrying a clipboard stopped by my cell. At first I thought he'd come for me. They'd discovered their mistake and were now going to transfer me. But my hopes quickly faded when he yanked the bars to my cell as though checking to be certain they were locked securely. Then, looking at his clipboard he asked me for my name.

"Excuse me, sir," I said, hoping he would notice that I was a mannerly person. "Is this what they call the disciplinary section?"

"Didn't you hear me ask you what your name is?" he said without expression.

At that, I figured if I answered his question, he might answer mine. "Altman," I replied, "A-L-T-M-A-N."

"What's you're number?"

"Just a moment. I have to look on this slip of paper. Haven't had a chance to memorize it yet. Here it is— B-55627."

The bull just looked at the clipboard and without looking up, turned and walked away. I heard him stop at the cell next door and ask the same name and number question—no matter how I pressed and strained at the bars—I couldn't see him. So I called out.

"Pardon me, sir. I know you're awfully busy—but would you be good enough to tell me—is this the disciplinary . . . ?"

Before I could finish he appeared in front of my cell. I hadn't heard him turn and walk back. And his appearance startled me. His drab olive uniform blended in with the rest of the drabness around me. His face looked as though any expression that might have been there had been sanded down to a frown and varnished. His mouth barely moved when he spoke.

"Look. We're right in the middle of 'count' and the rules are—no talking. I won't write you up this time—but I'm making a note of it."

He didn't write anything down. So I figured he meant a "note" in his head and I wondered how many little notes he carried there. But I thought as long as the bull was standing there, and as long as I wasn't going to get written up, I'd better ask my question. No telling when anyone would walk by again.

"I only wanted to know if this is the disciplinary block."

"I guess you've never been in the joint before, if you don't know. No, this isn't the 'hole.' This is your home. When you get off Fish Row in about five days—we'll assign you to a cell exactly like this one. Only you'll have company. We're crowded."

With that, the bull disappeared down the tier . . . "name and number . . . name and number . . . name . . ." He repeated automatically down the row of cells. I heard someone answer, "Bravo," and I said to myself why that wouldn't be Mike Bravo who went to P.S. 52 with me.

It wouldn't have surprised me. Of course, he was always into trouble—street rumbles, stealing cigarettes from Solomon's candy store, and what about that scene he caused in Mrs. Jammer's music class. She was a knockout. Mike sat in front of the classroom. Not because he was the smartest kid in our class, but Mrs. Jammer felt better having him within swatting distance. Anyway, Mike had a compact mirror and he discovered that if he held it at the proper angle, directed under the front of Mrs. Jammer's desk, he could get a glimpse up her dress. He'd gotten away with the mirror trick for a long time, and he'd always given us kids the report: "She ain't wearing none today. I could see the grass around Central Park . . . I couldn't see good, but I think they were blue . .. I ain't sure. . . ."

One day, having gotten away with this game for such a long time, Mike got brave. Mrs. Jammer was standing, her back to the class, writing on the blackboard. Mike figured if he taped the mirror to the tip of his shoe—he could steal up behind her and get a good view of "Central Park." So, there was Mrs. Jammer, swinging away with the chalk, the rest of us holding our breath while Mike sneaked up behind her. Mrs. Jammer must have been waiting because just as Mike slid the mirrored shoe directly under her, she dropped the chalk, swung around, and grabbed him by the ear. "Just what do you think you're doing?" she scowled. Mike's face flushed with astonishment. "I wasn't doin' nuthin', Mrs. Jammer," Mike whined. "Just tryin' to see the blackboard better."

"Since when is the blackboard underneath my dress—your

mother will hear about this!" She snapped, pointing to the mirror on his shoe. We kids erupted in howls of laughter. Even the girls. Even Angela Bochino—my childhood crush. Even she laughed . . .

I made a note—when I got off Fish Row—to check and see if it was the same Mike Bravo. If it were, wouldn't he be surprised to see "Fatso," the kid he called "sissy" because I refused to help him steal old man Solomon's cigarettes, here in Folsom Prison with him? Then I realized it couldn't be the same Mike Bravo because I'd heard or read somewhere that Mike had become a famous pop singer—changed his name and so forth—really made it big. Well, I made it big too. Can't get much bigger than Folsom Prison. What would Angela Bochino say if she could have seen me in that lifeless cell? Of course, she didn't know I had a crush on her. Not until the day Theresa and I visited New York after we were married, and we went to visit my old neighborhood. Angela had married. And when we visited her she was pregnant. I'll never forget her embarrassment. I told her that I used to leave the house early on Sundays just to watch her go to church with her parents. She looked so pretty in her white brocade Sunday dress and white straw hat with the pink ribbon trailing down her long dark hair. Oh, we'd been good friends. But I felt I was too fat for any girl to like me that way. So I never approached her, and she was really embarrassed when I showed her the heartshaped tattoo on my arm with her name on it. "Got it when I was in the Navy," I told her. Hey, Angela—look at me now. They got me stuck in a cell in prison. Well, I never tried to look up your dress, Angela. Or Mrs. Jammer's dress for that matter.

Being raised in Zayda's house along with mother's sisters I saw it all before I got to school. My aunts ran around the house in their underwear during bath time or when getting ready for dates and so forth. And, until I was ten years old, we all took baths together. I'd soap their backs, soap their titties all the marvelous parts of their bodies were for me no different than playing with my toys, and not even as interesting as that cherry-red fire truck with real lights and a silver bell that really rang.

Aunt Mitzi gave me that fire truck for my sixth birthday. She'd saved a whole year for it. The rest of the girls used to scold her for smothering and spoiling me. She'd just say. "It's my money. It's my nephew." Bathtime was fun. When Mitzi bathed me, she'd scrub me with yellow laundry soap and hot steamy water till my skin stung.

I never developed a curiosity about female anatomy—not with all those girls surrounding me. And by the time I entered kindergarten, all my exploring of the female anatomy had been accomplished. Thanks to mother's sisters. So, while Mike Bravo was looking for the "grass up in Central Park," I'd already found the water fountain in the mall.

Angela, I had the wildest crush on you without a thought about what was going on under your dress. My tattoo with your name is described on police records all over the country. And whenever I contemplated having it removed for a change of identity, I couldn't bring myself to have it done. And whenever booking officers noted the tattoo, I'd remember how we laughed when Mrs. Jammer caught Mike Bravo trying to look up her dress. But mostly, I remember how I loved you.

Those days on Fish Row, I recalled more about my lifetime than I had in over twenty years. The rapidity with which I was able to review my life reminded me that I had heard it said your whole life flashes before your eyes just before you die. Well, I wanted to be dead. I'd done such horrible things. I was disgusted and saturated with my lying and stealing and following an imaginary face and voice that constantly eluded me. So, I had reviewed my life and maybe I was dead.

And I wondered who would come to my funeral. Any of my wives? The women who thought they were married to a department store heir—never divorced one of them. Just disappeared . . . Any of the bankers I ripped off? They may come to the funeral—just to be sure I was really being buried for good. Maybe Theresa, my only legal wife, and my daughter, Terri. Maybe. . . .

One night I heard what sounded like a large group of teenagers—arguing back and forth from their cells shouting obscenities such as: "Yer mutha takes it in the mouth, muthafucka . . . when I fucked your mama I never thought we'd get a kid like you, who'd land in jail . . . I'm flushing' your mama down the shitter." Listening to them banter back and forth I worried over the fact that they allowed teenagers in Folsom Prison. I was told Folsom was only for older men—an end of the line "warehouse," and when on my first day off Fish Row I looked around for the youngsters—the gunsels. But all I could see were older men like myself. The youngest I'd judge to be around thirty years old—all moving around the prison quietly. Some, even arthritically. One, in a wheelchair, had to be seventy, at least.

I figured the teenagers I'd heard were just overnighters on their way to another joint. Until one night as Gordon and I left the mess hall an argument broke out behind us.

"Ah, yer mama sucks. . . ."

"Hey, I heard your mama's havin' her tongue removed— outa tha warden's asshole. . . ."

Now I'd find out who the teenagers were. When I turned around I was shocked to see two older men. They were in their fifties. They were arguing. It was them!

Old men. Moving like old men. Talking like children.

I didn't say a word to Gordon, on the way up to our cell. I began fitting the pieces together. These had to be people who'd been locked up since they were teenagers—or even before. These had to be the people who were destined by circumstance from the moment of their conception to go to jail. Maybe even born in jail. Born with a red mark. "Illegitimate kids," a bull said. "Shoulda bin born dead." I wanted to tell the bull that my Zayda said there was "no such thing as illegitimate children—only illegitimate, irresponsible parents." These were the people whose life had been shut off from the beginning. I thought about my own childhood. And Zayda, and Aunt Mitzi, and Theresa. And wondered why I had forced my way into prison. And wondered if I could come back to life again.

At least I had a meager semblance of a beginning. The first thirteen years of my life had been filled with a better than average home. My religious beliefs and life values, my Zayda saw to. I went to public and religious school daily. I had mountains of homework from both, which I did while listening to "The Lone Ranger," "The Shadow," "Mr. Keen—Tracer of Lost Persons," "Jack Armstrong—the All-American Boy."

I only had three absences in seven years. In *Chayda*, a good religious school, they gave me a certificate for attendance. Even Rabbi Katz signed it.

Anything with Rabbi Katz's signature was a treasure. "I don't endorse for one day's good behavior. When—and if—you graduate Hebrew school, people will ask what university you went to. If they don't ask you it's because you haven't learned to apply what we teach here."

Rabbi Katz was Jewish chaplain at Sing Sing Prison. And after he attended electrocutions he was not to be contended with. "We must vote against capital punishment. To put a man in prison for the rest of his natural life is a punishment worse than death." He'd say as he pointed an angry finger at the congregation. "Isn't that enough for you, my so-called highly evolved brothers? Or are you so steeped in the ferment of your own guilt, for your own shameful standards, that you still have need for the sacrificial goat? It is no more right for you to kill a man who has killed than it is for the man who kills. And so long as capital punishment exists we are teaching our children that to kill is right—and the solution to problems that would otherwise have alternatives. You and I may not live to see the word *kill* wiped away from the mentality of organized society, but if it is wiped out, then alternatives for the protection of peace will come about in natural order."

Hebrew school. Public school. Ten hours a day plus the mountains of homework for both. Though I didn't go past tenth grade until I went to prison, people have on occasion asked me what university I attended. I applied my knowledge to all of my con games. Applied it with skill.

And Zayda taught me how to swing a paint brush and handle tools. "In Rumania," he'd say, "we couldn't always get the right tools to repair a wheel or shoe a horse—so we had to make something else to do the work."

He was always inventing things to make "life easier" for Buba. And Buba would say, "Even ven ve vere children in de old country your Zayda vas dat vay. Alvays *patchkaing* around mit sumptin. He even carved for me a bracelet from vood—da whole ting links vitout en opening. Did I show you?"

So, I had the closeness, the love and caring of a family—and though it began to fall apart after my thirteenth birthday, I cannot forget it. Recalling the events until that time—even after my father moved in to Zayda's house when I was ten years old—gives me a feeling of warmth.

While my roots were pulled up early, in prison all around me were people who had no roots at all. Never had any. Not even a hint of education. Not even a trace of love. No one to kiss them. The walls, their mothers, the guntowers, their fathers. The bulls, the guards? They're the watchmen. The guards say who can visit the prisoners and who cannot—and sometimes prisoners expecting visitors don't know that visitors were there but got turned away. The bulls never let a prisoner know what's happening. Even if it affects the prisoner personally.

In jail, I was too wrapped up in my own case to pay close attention. But most of the people there had been going through reform schools, jails and prisons since before their teen years. And most just accepted it as a way of life. For most of these people, life on the streets was the punishment, and being sent away from a jail or prison was the same as being rejected by mother and father.

When I walked through the prison yard under the guntowers—prisoners working out on "Iron Piles"—weight lif-
ting, lining up for a movie on weekends, complaining if their
laundry came back too wrinkled, "It was better in Tracy,"
going about laughing, chatting about who's a snitch, "Watch
out for him," or who's been a "punk" (homosexual) since juvenile hall when he was ganged up on and raped, or that the
beans had more spice in San Quentin—I became aware that
almost all the prison population had known each other since
childhood, were raised together like brothers— and who indeed form "brotherhoods"—and who live by an unwritten
code more stringent and demanding than any law society can
impose upon itself—a code so exacting that to break it could
mean death. Strangely enough, the code demands: no lies, no
stealing (unless it's from the prison refrigerator), and, of
course, there's no girls.

I heard a lot of talk about "my old lady." And at first I
thought they were talking about girlfriends or mother. But I
soon found out that the "old ladies" were girls they'd been
raised in juvenile hall or an orphanage with—girls they
hadn't seen sometimes for thirty years or more.

Few of the men I met in Folsom had been "on the streets"
for more than a year since they were kids. And by the time
they reached Folsom Prison that could mean over sixty years.
Then, there were some who'd been locked up from the very
moment they breathed life. And the world "outside" was as
remote to them as my grandparents' Rumania or Mitzi's stars
were to me.

For some I met, homosexuality is a way of life. A way to
release sexual energy. And some have even been "married"
since they were kids. Occasionally, on a Sunday, you might
see a small group gathered in a corner of the yard. And if you
get close enough you can be witness to a double-ring marriage ceremony between two male convicts. Dead serious.
And once in a while a "couple" will go to the prison chaplain
for "Pre-marriage Counseling." "We wanna get married.
Settle down. Get out of all these hassles in the yard,

Chaplain." How'd you like to be the chaplain?

Of the "married" couples, the one who grows into the masculine role, supports and protects his "woman." The money he earns in the license plate factory is spent at the canteen for their household needs—and once in a while a gift such as a giant Hershey's chocolate bar or bag of cookies. But gifts mainly come in the form of a nifty leather belt, billfold or even a purse. And if the "man" of the family does not have the talent for making these items, any of which his "old lady" can be nagging him for, he will buy them with cigarettes (the major means of barter) or trade "hotdog" books (*Playboy*, *Penthouse* and so forth) or a small cabinet he made in the handicraft shop.

It's not unusual for an "old lady" to swish up and down the tiers, hallways, and yard, flaunting some bauble at the other "queens" saying, gleefully, "See what my husband gave me for our anniversary!"

And they receive the same compliments and behind-the-back cattiness that women on the streets get from their friends.

If you make a pass at "her" or her "husband" you would have done better to commit suicide. The end results most assuredly will be the same, unless you go into protective custody with Charles Manson. And if you go into protective custody voluntarily you'll get a label that could get you killed by someone who is not in "P.C." voluntarily.

By the time these "couples" reach Folsom Prison, it's likely they've gone through their dating games in one of the other joints, and their commitments to each other are sealed—rings and all. Some have been killed for in the yards of San Quentin, Tracy, and Attica and so forth. Riots can be caused over a "queen" just as easily as rotten prison conditions or racism.

People such as myself, "first termers," are not invited into any of the family groups—or brotherhoods. Not unless they know you, or of you, will you be invited to a "wedding."

That was okay with me. I'd put out untold streams of energy just to become invisible. I spent half a lifetime devising methods of moving about the world unnoticed—and one time I even tried to become invisible through the use of magical incantations. Black Magic. Well, it worked. Because you cannot be any more invisible than you are in prison. In fact, it becomes a tremendous, sometimes heartbreaking struggle to hold on to a flimsy thread of identity.

XV

"The 'Book of Deaths' is easy to find," said Sgt. Barker, the hospital bull. It was my first day off Fish Row and I'd been assigned as clerk in the prison hospital, and Sergeant Barker, my supervisor, was directing me to the location of the "Book of Deaths."

"Just as you walk into the second floor office, turn left and you'll see it . . . can't miss it . . . right on top of the four-drawer file cabinet—the one marked "Autopsy Reports." It's one o' them green ledger books . . . sort of faded—worn around the edges—anyway the cover is marked in red crayon: 'Folsom Prison Book of Deaths.' Gotta have it right away . . . enter that stickin' we had in the yard this morning . . . Son-of-a-bitch didn't make it. Time wasn't up either. Guess we'll have to bury him standing up, till his time's done (ha-ha). Anyway, Altman . . . Altman . . . Altman . . . ," he pondered, "Did have an Altman here 'bout thirty years ago when I started to work here—any relation?"

"No, sir," I said, "Not as far as I know."

"Don't have to call me *sir*," he said, "Sarge is good enough. Earned my stripes. Yes, sir, really earned them. Anyway, Sarge'll do. In a few years—when you get to know me—you can call me Barker. And if you keep your nose clean, I'll let you take a sandwich and cookies back to your cell at night. One of the privileges o' workin' for me. Now, g'wan and get that book. I'm going down to the medication window. See you back there."

Finding the "Book of Deaths" I thumbed through it. I felt queasy. It was a thick ledger book filled with mug shots and statistics of the guys that had been hung there, or those who killed themselves or killed by a bull or an inmate or died of natural causes. And I wondered how many of them were "buried standing up."

Feeling nauseated, I tucked the book under my arm and carried it back to Sergeant Barker at the medication window. There was a crowd of big bulls carrying billy clubs surround-

150

ing a short, emaciated prisoner standing by the window. "Stand back," one of the bulls commanded me. I froze. One of the bulls poured some Maalox into a paper cup, handed it to the prison. "If you start eatin' right you won't need this shit."

"The only way you'll get me to eat is to let me out of protective custody—or force-feed me."

Then the group of bulls left with the prisoner. "Who was that?" I asked Sergeant Barker as I handed him the book.

"Charlie boy."

"Charlie boy?"

"Yeah. Charley Manson."

Manson: Tate Murders. Altman: Con man—bad checks. Same prison. I excused myself, went to the toilet and threw up.

Something was said about my being too weak to work in the hospital. There was an opening as clerk for the Jewish chaplain. I was transferred.

One day I asked the canteen manager if he could order *matzos* and *gefilte-fish*. "Nope," he said, dead serious, "not enough Jews here to make it pay. Besides, doesn't the rabbi bring that shit in?" The Jewish chaplain—who I worked for—did bring those items in for us on the Jewish holidays. Rabbi Ehrnkrantz would "discover" unwritten holidays. He'd confess to our small congregation: "A good, kosher salami and some *halavah* can maybe become a tiny glow in these dark halls of horror. So what if it's not a traditional holiday. Isn't anything that happens good here a holiday?"

Because the rabbi visited only once a week I depended on Jim McGee, the full-time Protestant chaplain for such things as supplies for the Jewish office and "emergency" phone calls home for our small congregation. We managed about one five-minute phone call a month per man.

Considering the telephone is the main means of communication, five minutes a month is not a hell of a lot. Not really. Not when you're locked in a tiny cell from three in the afternoon until six o'clock the following morning. Sixteen hours a day in a cage equipped with a toilet, a sink and a bunk. A cage in which you can stand up, stretch your arms, and touch the walls with your fingertips. I could do that. I did that a lot. I'm built small. Don't have a long reach at all. I have to stand on a chair to get stuff out of the top shelves in the kitchen. But I could touch those cell walls with my fingertips.

Most of the time we were forced into double-celling: cramming two men into a tiny cage. It's hard enough alone. But if you're alone you don't have to worry about being killed over snoring too loud or flushing the toilet when your "partner" is trying to sleep. The homosexuals like double-celling. And the administration encourages it by not preventing it. But for guys that hold on to the memory of how beautiful a woman's behind can be, having another man's ass in your face for sixteen hours a day for days, months, years without seeming end can irritate the shit out of you. And it can really shake you when his ass begins to look good.

But if it wasn't for double-celling I wouldn't have met Gordon Kirkwood-Yates. Gordon is in prison for murder. Gordon beat a drunk to death. It was at a party. This fellow kept pawing at Gordon's wife all night. Gordon warned the slob to stop. Several times. The last warning brought Gordon a fist in the mouth. Gordon hit him with a blow to the head. The drunk fell, hitting his head on the corner of a coffee table. He died.

Unfortunately for Gordon the man he hit in self-defense and in defense of his wife happened to be a United States prosecuting attorney. The charge should have been manslaughter at the most. But because everyone at that party had been drinking heavily no one could come up with a fact that could help Gordon. Everyone claimed they hadn't noticed the events that led up to the fight. In fact no one could swear who hit who first. So, Gordon, who had up to that moment taught school and lived quietly with his wife and daughter in a suburb of Los Angeles, went to prison for murder. "She must have encouraged him," Gordon confided to me, "I figure that because it didn't take her long to divorce me after I got locked down. Got married right away too. . . ."

When Gordon and I became cellmates I had heard only that he was there for killing a man. And since violence had never been my thing—I was a swindler, a con man—I was damned nervous and upset over being locked down with him. But as it turned out, our relationship grew close, and meaningful. He taught me how to shape a poem, we talked about our families, our children, and the life we led before prison. We played chess, read and wrote poetry, and spent long hours writing to family and writers outside. When we got mail from anyone we shared the contents with each other. And with the sharing we became close friends.

And for the first time since I began my twenty years of bilking banks, six marriages without benefit of divorce, and running up and down the map of the United States and Mexico, I began to think. I asked myself why I took a red felt-tip pen and marked my face with long angry strokes. Gordon looked at me. He stayed calm. And in a steady, even voice said, "Wash that shit off your face, you're getting the crazies, Irwin, write a poem about it."

I heard him. And I was aware that what I'd done with the pen was crazy. But I was worried and frustrated. Only three weeks before the red pen incident I went before the parole board to ask to go home. And they hadn't yet given me the results of my hearing.

When I appeared in front of the board, California's indeterminate-sentence law was still in effect. And even if the crime was not major—petty theft, bad checks and so forth, crimes that called for sentences of a minimum of a year to a maximum of fourteen years—we never knew, until the "board" decided, when we were going home. There was no way to plan for a future. No way to know how long you'd be locked in a cage. It could be one year. It could be fourteen years. It could be never. Or if the sentence called for five years to life—you could stay in prison until you died. Some men and women did die in prison while waiting for a panel of people to decide their fate. And some of those men and women had been imprisoned for nothing more than smoking grass. Smoking it—not peddling it!

Considering that the panel of gods—the parole board members—are sitting there drawing thirty-seven-thousand dollars a year, for no reason other than they control a block of the taxpayers' vote, or contributed handsomely to a political campaign or both, the total concept becomes frightening. It is additionally frightening if any of the people on the panel have political aspirations. Looks good in the newspapers to keep criminals in prison. Even first offenders. I met people in prison who are perhaps in their forties who went to prison at age eighteen for burglary. Twenty-two years! And they are first offenders. No, they didn't kill anyone in prison. But when you're an eighteen-year-old thrown in prison with a one-to-fifteen year sentence it's damned hard not to get into a fight or two. Each fight can add a few years to the sentence. Sometimes, the prison officials will take a convict to court and charge him with assault which can put several years onto the existing sentence.

When the panel does give a release date some convicts lockdown and don't venture out to the yard until time to go home. They just go out to the mess hall for meals. Reason? Just in case you walked into a fight or a stabbing—you could be blamed. You could lose your release date. Convict code: "Always walk away from a dying man."

It was after I'd appeared in front of the parole panel that I had that attack of the crazies and marked my face up. Three weeks had gone by without my receiving the "board results." And even though Jim McGee had assured me, "You'll make it, Irwin. Three-and-a-half years is enough for a bad check— more than enough. You'll get a parole."

Crossing the yard back to the cell block my thoughts were on the board decision would be. The warning whistle blew as I entered the cell block. And I remember getting paranoid over telling Jim McGee about being a hairdresser at one time. "But, shit, he knows I'm not geared," I told myself. "And he doesn't know about that night I got turned on to Gordon. Gordon doesn't know either. Thank my fucking Christ!"

Whenever Gordon and I got tired of writing and reading we'd play chess. Sometimes until morning. In the summer the cells were always too hot so we sat on the lower bunk (Gordon's) in our shorts. Gordon said, "Damn, I wish we had a Monopoly game."

"Yeah. Shit. My friends and I used to play Monopoly a lot when we were kids," I said.

"We did too, man. My mother used to pretend that those little wooden hotels were Scottish castles her family had brought over brick by brick. We'd interrupt the game while mother told us stories about the family farm in Scotland. Someday I want to write about that. But not here. I don't want to bring her that close to this fucking joint. In fact, Irwin, you're the only one I discuss my family with."

"Same here, man; if it weren't for you and Jim McGee and the Rabbi, I'd of probably jumped off the top tier, or climbed the wall just so they'd shoot me down. It's the first time since I've been a kid I've allowed myself a close friendship. Shit, Gordon, I don't even know how to be a friend anymore. Too many years chasin' rainbows. Fuckin' people around. People that had nothing to do with causing me to get fucked up in the first place. No way to make it up to those people either."

"Irwin, if you really care, you'll straighten out. Hard to tell from prison. Man'll say anything to get out. If you get out and come back and I'm still here, I'll kick your ass. And if I'm not here I'll leave word with Pancho or Ernie. And as for this shit about your not knowing how to be a friend—just what the hell do you think you are to me? What else have we shared except our lives in this hole. What about our plans to open a coffeehouse for writers. You are a writer now, you know. It's a heavy trip, writing. Because if you're lying, it shows up on paper. But if you spill your natural guts—even if you call if fiction—it'll be felt. People'll say, "God damn, that's got to be based on experience." They'll know because they're in this fucked-up world with you, Irwin. Some just handle it differently. Another thing, after all the work I've put in teaching you a few writing skills—if you don't write—I'll be disappointed."

"We'll have our coffee shop. Maybe feed some hungry poets. I might be one of them."

As we were talking I was reminded of the days of the four freaks. And it struck me that my friendship with Gordon was not much different than that I had with the freaks when I was a kid. Gordon and I shared everything. We emptied our guts to each other. So I looked at Gordon—sitting on the bunk in our shorts, in our "house," locked in like the freaks did years ago in Zayda's wine cellar—and I wanted those days back again. And when Gordon mentioned wanting a Monopoly game the memory of my childhood filled me. And I remembered that when we freaks were in our shorts we'd jack each other off. And that's what I wanted to do with Gordon. And the urge scared the shit out of me. I stuffed it and said, "You know, when I was a kid I belonged to a club . . ."

"Oh, yeah," Gordon interrupted, "the four freaks. You told me about them. Kids do crazy things, don't they."

"Yeah, man," I said over a deep sigh of relief, "kids sure get into crazy things."

On the stairwell up to my tier I remember looking at the fellows around me. We all looked the same. Same wrinkled blues. Same expressionless faces. A sad sea of blue wrinkles emptying into their cells for the night. I wondered how many were geared to suck pricks. Maybe someone was wondering about me. Maybe I wanted someone to wonder about me. Everything had such a final sameness. Blue sameness.

Sometimes there was blood on the sea. Whenever someone got knifed their blood would spurt on whoever was nearby. A blue sea of blood, splashing against the walls, into the cells, foaming around the base of the white toilets. Human being reduced to bubbles of blood. Human beings reduced to graffiti on the toilet walls of the parole board, human beings reduced to microfilm statistics projected on the warden's viewing screen.

Eyes: fixed, frozen, staring at a man jumping off the top tier—head first. Was it because he didn't get a letter from home or was it that he was afraid he might suck a prick or want to suck a prick. Father, bless me father, for I have sinned. I had a desire to suck a prick . . . no I didn't, father . . . is wanting to the same kind of sin as doing it? What? Oh no. Father. Not since I was a kid playing with my friends in Zayda's wine cellar . . . you won't tell the parole board will you, father? . . . please I want to go home . . , home . . . wait, I'm not a Catholic, I can't confess. Is eating your aunt's pussy the same sin as wanting to suck a prick?

"Irwin, I said wash that red shit off your face before the bull walks by. He's due any minute."

I could hear Gordon, but couldn't snap out of it. I knew I was having an attack of the crazies. We all got them. But they're hard to control.

"Irwin, God damn it, man, the bull's walking. Snap out of it, man!"

I felt Gordon grab me by the shoulders and spin me around so that I faced the sink. I heard the water splash. Felt a hot soapy towel rub against my face. A brusque drying. "Staring into space again," I said.

"Yeah, man. You must have been on a hell of a trip. What were you tripping on—eating pussy?"

The bell rang. The topbar slid back, releasing the door to our cell, and just as we pushed the cell door open, a bull walked by. He was shuffling a stack of mail. "Altman, you got a couple of letters. Looks like one's from the parole board."

I stuck the letters in my back pocket and didn't look at them until we got back from the mess hall. Sure. I wanted to know what the board had to say. But I was afraid to open the letter. Finally, I did. And after reading it over several times, being absolutely certain I had it down right, I said to Gordon, "I'm going home in March. Five months to go!"

And that night, sitting cross-legged on my bunk—a million thoughts swam through my mind. Home. Home? Write a poem. If Zayda were alive he'd take pleasure in a poem I wrote. Remembering Zayda, the old neighborhood, Mother, the words—my first poem—began to flow:

My eyes, like brown brickchips—baked-clay mirrors, reflect tenement-youth days where my brain was whittled by the hollow wailing of wrinkled, bony, old men chanting chilling prayers— desperate words—written long ago on parchment scrolls across burning deserts.

Countless are the days since my warm child-breath wove frosted daydreams upon winters' misty windows. Haunting memories, are the bearded beggars who sang for crusts of bread or copper coin. Pain seeking salve in pain. Hunger calling to the hungry. A slice of bread. A penny. A cup of steaming soup.

Ragged souls. Weary. Frozen voices bent like fading neon signs. They hawked their wares of despair.

"Used clothes for sale . . ."

"Pots and pans . . ."

"Razorblades . . ."

"Old keys for sale . . ."

"A penny a penny," they'd cry—then, die another step into too many tomorrows.

Yes, the cries were many. But, for me, there were none like the one who sold old keys. His rippling white beard whipped in the winter wind. His eyes revealed picture-puzzle years— blue, jigsaw pieces of a life never fitting.

No. There were none like the one with his old-world chant: "Ayleeee . . . Ayleeee . . . Hay-ay-ayleeee . . . lo-ho-o . . . haz- aftoneeee . . . Ayleeee . . . Ay-hay-ayleeee . . . lo-ho-o-haz-ahftoneeee . . . Lord . . . Lord . . .why hast thou forsaken me. . . ."

He'd chant, mystically, as he rattled his ring of keys toward the skies. And in his trembling voice I could hear the distant, warning roar of falling templestones. Stones of tangled time.

"M'shuga . . . crazy!" my mother would say. "Whoever hoid of selling old keys? Vy don't he sell sumting people could use?—Like old shoes! Listen, you shouldn't give him anyting . . . you hear? Not enyting!"

Ayleeee . . . Ayleeee . . .

Now he's gone. The years have passed. I remember how sad was the day he died. He lay on the sidewalk, limp—like a bundle of rags. I remember the circle of curious people gathered around him.

They stared. They wondered. But they didn't care. Not really. I looked on in grieving disbelief and tightly clutched the key I'd bought the day before. I cried inside when someone asked his name. Didn't they know? A woman among them said, "That's old Peter . . . you know . . . he sold keys that didn't fit anything . . . crazy. . . ."

I turned my back to the callous crowd and walked away; quietly remembering: "Ayleeee . . . Ayleeee. . . ."

Now, I gaze back through the fleeting years. And, from an old trunk filled with mementoes of the treasured past, I dig out a dented cookie box. It's filled with keys I've saved along with the memory of his smiling words to me: "Someday, you'll think of me and say, 'The keys of Solomon are mine.' "

> I am a tattered beggar—
> —a hungry beggar
> seeking meat
> from the mouths of
> cloistered monks,
> I am a blind beggar—
> a weary beggar seeking light
> from the eyes of shadows
> beneath chapel walls. . . .

More than anything I wanted to write. Write skillfully. Give something of value and even entertain people. So, when I received my first critique, I said thank you. Then, in the privacy of my own head I said: "You son-of-a-bitch." Still I knew it was right. That's why I was so fucking angry. Angry enough to remember father's funeral. Angry enough to remember the ruby ring. Angry enough to remember the gold watch. And I felt anger toward myself for defrauding the world and trampling on the feelings of the women who'd thought they had a husband. Then it struck me. I was angry. I could feel the hot piss of anger steaming through my veins. I could feel again. When was the last time I felt anything real? I had a *real* feeling. A feeling I could touch. In my moment of anger one of the friendlier bulls walked by my cell. I gripped the bars. "Hey, look at me!" I said, "I'm angry—really angry!"

"Need something from the dispensary to calm you down?"

"No. Hell, no. I don't need anything. Not a thing. Think I'll write a poem for my father."

"Still writing that poetry stuff—huh?"

"Better than pissing my time away in the yard."

"Yeah, true. Well, at least you're not one of them radical socialists—I mean after all—you know you live in America." The friendly bull yanked my bars to be sure they were locked, and walked down the tier yanking bars along the way.

My cell in "America" no longer fit. Still, I was locked in. Going over in my mind what the bull had said about poetry I recalled a few lines from A. D. Winan's "A Bicentennial Poem":

> The bicentennial drums roll
>   along
> The magic ohm of Ginsberg
>   buried
> Deep in the ass of an
> Arab camel driver who doesn't
> Know the difference between
> A poem and a dollar . . .

The five months dragged. I was sweating out the federal government's answer as to whether or not they'd go along with the state's recommendation that I be paroled. And as my state release date drew closer, my tension mounted. Four years is enough for bad checks. The only reason the feds were involved was that I had transported the checks across the state line into California, where I'd passed them. For that I got four years to run together with my fourteen-year state sentence. I hadn't been prosecuted for the bigamies. The women, much to the aggravation of the states involved, didn't want to appear against me, and didn't want publicity. So, all was clear. Except for the eight months.

Finally, I'd cut it down to the last three nights and my muscles were so tense I had difficulty walking. So, I stayed in the cell on my bunk waiting for the answer from the federal government. The only thing I did was go out for evening meals with Gordon.

On the third day a con nicknamed "Cuntjuice" hung himself. He got the nickname because every time he got a letter from his wife he'd wave it in front of any nose he could. "Smell it, man!" Cuntjuice would beam, "She rubbed it on her you-know-what." Sure. He was simple. Sure. But doing life or any kind of prison time can do even worse things to a human being.

The hanging was more than I could cope with. And my last night there, on the way back from dinner I was overcome with the crazies: the mind's escape from maddening reality. I feed the gutter rats plenty of bread and fruit each afternoon before lockup in hopes they'll stay away from my cell. I think: only one more night before I go home, maybe . . . hope I don't get bitten by a rat. Die from rabies. By the time I reach my cell I talk myself in and out of a case of rabies. I stretch out on my bunk. Talk to myself aloud. "No, Irwin," I console myself, "It's not likely. They may be lowly rats. But they know who feeds them."

I wonder how many times I've flushed my toilet in the four years I've been here. I try to figure it out but stop at the count of ten. Four years in Folsom for swindling a bank. Well, I can take one more night. Look at Carl, next door. He'll be here forever. No escape, except for the crazies.

One day! Maybe. The thought excites and worries me. I can't fall asleep. What if something goes wrong? What if the government doesn't let me go? Can't let my feelings show. Don't want the guys to laugh at me. For now I'll keep my feelings stuffed and tightly capped. But in just one day when I turn my back to the walls and towers and gunwalks; when I'm safely away from the scrutiny of the bulls, I'll greet the world with ringing howls of relief.

For now I'll stuff it. Be still. Wait for welcome sleep to quiet me. Can't figure out if I'm dozing or slipping into the crazies. Maybe I'm beginning to dream. Doesn't matter. I see the small round figure of my mythical mother—the mother I made up when I was a kid. The mother mine could never be. The mother that would take pride in her son—no matter what . . . Look, she's sitting with her *yenta* friend Ethel. They're in Canter's Delicatessen. There's the waitress bringing them coffee and bagels . . .

"So tell me, Bertie, what's new?" Ethel asks mother in hopes of getting the latest goings-on.

"What could be new that you don't already know, Ethel," mother says. "I thought maybe you could tell me."

Ethel folds her hands over her coffee cup. Her brown eyes light up. "Oy, could I tell you," says Ethel, pleased to get the first word. "Did I tell you the latest about my little Bernie the doctor?"

Ethel, sounding like a parrot, is bragging endlessly about Bernie's successes . . . Bernie's wife . . . Bernie's children . . . Bernie's new house. . . .

"Listen, Ethel!" says mother, interrupting impatiently. "Let me tell you about my son, Irwin, the thief." Enjoying Ethel's register of shock, mother continues without stopping. "He, my son, my little Irwin, just swindled a big bank and ran off to South America with a *shicksa!*"

Now I know it's the crazies. Mother and Ethel fade from mind and a different scene unfolds. I seem to be standing naked in the middle of the prison dress-out shack. I'm surrounded by a circle of three men and three green-eyed women. They're dressed up like cheerleaders at a football game. They're all wearing blue turtleneck sweaters. The men wearing white slacks, the women showing white pleated skirts. A large, white letter "F" is sewn to the front of their sweaters. One of the women in the circle points toward my groin and announces: "See! I told you his balls are missing." I'm afraid to look down.

"Irwin," says one of the men, "where the hell are your balls? We've come to weigh them. Can't let you go home until we weigh your balls . . . Lift your prick up—Let's see those balls—got to check your balls—you came in with them—and even though they're not quite the same—we gotta make 'em look that way before you go . . . Don't worry about the women seeing your prick—you probably can't use it anymore anyway. . . ." I know that they exist only to my peculiar imagination . . . imagination number: B-55627. I know it's only my own crazy thoughts fucking with my head when I can swear that someone in the circle tells me that my newly issued, real clothes, especially those baggy pants on the bench, don't fit right. "You gotta go naked. . . ."

Hey! Didya hear? Cuntjuice just hung himself . . . Well, anyway the food's good . . . Hey! Didya hear? Altman's gone home! Home . . . Saw him myself . . . Walkin' out the gate . . . I was on the garbage run . . . His street pants were really baggy—long . . . caught under his heels . . . looked funny . . . yeah, funny. . . .

So, with the two-hundred dollars in my pocket, I turned my back to Folsom Prison, filled with hope and new friends. I headed for San Francisco, and Theresa, my only legal wife. I'd walked out on her twenty years before I went to prison, and except for a few brief encounters we had not seen each other during that time. And though she's explained why she waited, why she raised our daughter Terri alone, and while I am grateful that she never filed for a divorce, I don't believe I'll ever really understand.

When I walked through the door of our apartment and took Theresa in my arms, it was as though I'd never left. And standing there, happy to be out of prison, happy to be home, happy to have Theresa in my arms, but wondering if I'd be able to stay in one place.

Gordon Kirkwood-Yates, Poet Prisoner
Folsom Prison, California

Dear Gordon:

I have kept my promise. Here is the book.
I am planning a vacation to New York. Then, I'll go to
Coney Island, take a stroll on the boardwalk, stop at the spot
between the steeplechase and the funhouse, turn my gaze
toward planet Lam and wave goodbye to Mitzi.

Love,

Irwin

San Francisco